Great, Just Great!

Paris bound, country bred.

HELEN ROW TOEWS

VOLUME TWO

Printed in North America
First edition, Volume Two, 2020

Great, Just Great!
Volume Two

Edited by Jennifer D. Foster, a Toronto, Canada-based
freelance editor, writer, mentor and owner of Planet Word
http://lifeonplanetword.wordpress.com/

Cover design by Todd Toews

The names and identifying details of some characters in this book have
been changed. Also, in the story, "An Uncultured Lout," no disrespect
is intended to the artist or their work. The opinions stated are merely
those of a simple country girl, uneducated, unrefined and glad of it.

myprairiewool.com

This book is dedicated to my grandson Kayden
for all the sleepovers, silliness and fun.

ACKNOWLEDGMENTS

I would like to thank a few people without whom this book would not be possible.

First of all my husband Tom for his love and understanding as he puts up with my long hours at the computer.

The family and friends who allowed their stories to be told, and for their constant encouragement: Deborah, Susan, Arthetta, Cindy M. and Lori, to name only a few.

Daughter Aliyah for reading each story over before it goes to print, even though she whines about it.

My stepson Todd Toews for his artistic expertise in creating the cover and helping me in many other ways too numerous to mention. These books could not have been done without you.

Melanie Toews, my step-daughter-in-law for all of her support and kindness.

Anna Toews for her fresh ideas and sweet heart.

Gwen Muskego for believing in me, especially when I don't believe in me. You are a gem and I'm proud to call you friend.

Cyndi Rasmussen for the times of collaboration, advice and sharing of fun. For reading all that I ask and telling me ever so gently where it needs to be changed. Bless you.

My wonderful editor, Jennifer Foster that I feel so grateful to have found. Thank you for your wisdom, advice and for all the hours of work you put into polishing my tales. Your knowledge has been invaluable. Having you along for the ride has meant more than I can say.

And finally, love and thanks always go to Dad. He shall ever be my inspiration and my rock. I am who I am because of you.

Love you Dad.

TABLE OF CONTENTS

Affairs of the Heart 7

A Roman Adventure 10

A Roman Adventure (Part Two) 13

Beaver Tales 16

Bon Appetit! 19

Gesundheit! 23

Great, Just Great! 26

Never A Dull Moment 29

The Magic of Spring 33

Green Thumbs 36

It Could Be Worse 39

Two Wheels That Move the Soul 42

First Jobs 45

Travel is a Great Teacher 48

What's Sense Got to Do With It? 51

Congratulations! 54

Real Riches 57

Dream or Nightmare? 60

Making Memories 63

A Country Wave 66

Meeting the Folks 69

My Sincerest Apologies 72

Birthday Bash 75

Business Blunders 78

An Uncultured Lout 81

The Young and the Foolish 84

Necessary Evils/Finding Love 87

Hoarding	90
Stick 'Em Up!	93
The Truth Will Set You Free	96
Care to Dance	99
Two Simple Truths	102
Exercise Has Come a Long Way, Baby	105
Good Taste?	108
Where the Wild Things Go	111
The Family That *Slays* Together, *Stays* Together	114
A Burning Desire	117
Budget Travel 101	120
Kind Words	123
Gotta Love 'Em	126
Start Your Engines	129
Learning From Our Mistakes	132
What A Game!	137
Things That Go *Squeak*	141
Many Thanks	145
A Place in the Sun	148
Holiday Rituals	151
A Christmas Carol	155
Oh, Christmas Tree	158
Christmas on the Ranch	161

Dear Reader,

Lest you think I have lost my writer's way, compiling a mishmash of disjointed stories without sense or reason, I would like to explain that they were written over the course of two years as newspaper columns, where skipping about from subject to subject was encouraged.

These tales are lighthearted and intended to brighten my reader's day. In a world where we are daily bombarded with trouble and worry from every quarter, my fondest wish is that these stories bring each of you a smile.

Helen

Affairs of the Heart

Does age matter when it comes to affairs of the heart? Certainly not. This week, a friend showed me recent pictures of her uncle and his new bride. He's eighty-two. He and his betrothed had been childhood sweethearts, who reconnected after losing touch some fifty years earlier. Romantic, right?

Of course, all relationships don't begin or end as happily. So, for those fine men hoping to meet a special someone, I have taken the liberty of compiling a handy guide, complete with real-life examples. You're welcome.

Many rendezvous begin over a steaming beverage in the nonthreatening atmosphere of a coffeehouse. But what if the fellow you meet was like the man I was introduced to? He spoke for two solid hours on one subject—tires!

Let's be clear on one thing: that's not a date, it's a monologue. I mean, it was restful, since I wasn't required to participate beyond an occasional nod, but, as a general rule, monologues are desperately dull, particularly ones concerning steel-belted rubber.

He debated the minimum tread depth required for winter driving, waxed eloquent over air pressure, and knowledgeably discussed road conditions, climate interference, and the misuse of a manufacturer's warranty. Finally, at the conclusion of our visit, with misty eyes, he declared his undying love for the Goodyear family (Who knew tire lovers were such a close-knit group?) and then produced pictures of a new set he'd acquired using the company's finance program. Sigh.

Tip Number One: Leave the soliloquys with Shakespeare, where they belong. Go out on a limb and ask a girl a few questions. It's nice to share information on your hobby, but two hours' worth is preposterous.

I'd been seeing a fellow for a couple of weeks when Valentine's Day rolled around, and he popped over to my place with a present, telling me proudly he'd asked the help of a saleswoman when making this important purchase. I was impressed. Breathlessly, he presented me with a gorgeous gift wrapped in thin pink tinfoil, tied with matching bows and ribbons.

I envisioned what must certainly lurk within. Was it bath salts and fragrant soaps? Perhaps a lovely perfume, or a book and slippers with which to pamper myself? Holding my breath, I slowly pulled the paper away, savoring the moment as the outside of the box was revealed and I saw the manufacturer.

Wait a minute. Did Proctor Silex ever make women's beauty products? Nope. I lifted the gift from the wrapping paper with astonishment. It was a bathroom scale with a durable metal platform and solid foot grips—how . . . touching.

This "present" gives rise to several interesting questions. Whatever happened to flowers and chocolates? Was he delivering a not-so-subtle and unappreciated hint? What kind of nut was this aforementioned saleswoman? And who, in their right mind, would want to clamber onto a weigh scale for Valentine's Day, or be reminded of the excess poundage they'd put on over Christmas?

Tip Number Two: Household appliances rarely make appropriate gifts—romantic or otherwise. It doesn't have to be expensive, but almost any sort of present is better than a bathroom scale.

Of course, this was a forgivable faux pas, and when he invited me to his home next day for brunch, I accepted with a smile. However, as I seated myself at the kitchen table and viewed the food preparations, it was all I could do not to bolt for the door.

After reaching into the refrigerator, he produced a box of frozen waffles. This, in and of itself is not unusual, but then he stood at the counter, briskly slashing at them with a serrated knife. A pale, greenish haze accompanied this endeavor, and I craned my head in curiosity. With infinite care, he bent over each toaster treat, shaving a thick growth of *mold* from their sides. *Horrors!*

Tip Number Three: Raw, unadulterated penicillin is not breakfast food! No one expects culinary excellence, but serving a meal derived from a box of decomposing waffles will almost certainly breed contempt, not love. Also, it lent a whole new meaning to the slogan, "L'eggo my Eggo."

And there you have it, folks: a few pointers to ponder for Valentine's Day! Have a good one.

A Roman Adventure

Winter break for teachers and students is right around the corner. Some folks head for a warmer climate, but my friend Cindy M. and I once walked the ancient streets of Rome during this icy February break. I thought I'd tell you a little of our adventure, plus include several travel tips that could apply when visiting any overseas country.

My first tip would be to scout out the look of your lodgings ahead of time via the Internet and check out the nearby streets, so you know the area. There are always a few taxi drivers in any big city who will take advantage of tourists suffering from jet lag and feeling overwhelmed. We caught the late-night train into Rome from the airport, but didn't feel like trudging the many blocks to our rental. We called a cab.

I'm not sure if he purposely meant to drive us all around the vicinity for extra fare, or if he honestly missed our turn, but thanks to Google Street View, I had scoped it all out beforehand and knew exactly where we were. As he shifted gears, rushing past our street in a flurry of dry leaves and loud Italian music, I leaned forward and pointed it out.

"*Scusa, signora,*" he smiled, deftly wheeling the small car around and heading back.

My next pointer involves mistakes that can be made when translating a foreign language. The morning after our arrival, I left my friend sleeping and went out to explore. The sky was a bright, icy blue and the air crisp as I wandered the narrow cobbled streets, ducking under branches bent low with unwanted oranges. What a change from the frigid Canadian Prairies.

Spying a *negozio di alimentari* (grocery store), I popped in to buy coffee, fresh fruit, warm ciabattas, and a small pat of butter. *Won't Cindy be pleased when she awakes to find breakfast,* I thought gladly. However, purchasing groceries or items in a drugstore is always a little risky when it's in a different language. Obviously, I knew what bread looked like and I could smell the coffee, but cream and butter took a bit of guesswork, especially without my translator.

Nonetheless, now back at our rented apartment, I forgot all about it as Cindy seated herself at the table to eat, while I prepared our hot drinks in the kitchen.

"This stuff tastes weird," she called presently. "It may be some type of cheese, but it's sure not butter."

A cold hand of fear clenched at my heart, as I returned to see her trustingly take another bite of the tan-colored, somewhat-crumbly mixture she'd spread thickly on her bread. Noting the words written across the package, *"Lievito di birra,"* I quickly consulted the pocket translator I'd forgotten to take with me earlier.

"STOP!" I hollered, as she raised the bun to her lips once more. "You're eating brewer's yeast!"

The lesson here is twofold: keep some sort of language

translator on your person at all times and maintain a sense of humor. Things will always go wrong, but if you can take it in stride, your trip will go much more smoothly.

Forgiveness and understanding are great qualities, too. Not everyone could ingest half a package of compressed yeast on their morning bun and laugh about it, but she did.

Happily, we made up for it by strolling the bustling streets of Rome, sitting at a small sidewalk café to enjoy frothy cappuccinos and wandering through a lively market. I've been grateful for every travel adventure I've had. If you keep an open mind and a keen eye, you can't help but improve your travel know-how.

One of the real benefits of travel, though, lies in our ability to see and experience how other folks live and to find we aren't so different after all.

Standing on a spot that bore the feet of those who helped shape who we are as a people today gives one pause. It leaves not only a sense of how insignificant each one of us is, but also of how connected.

And that is priceless.

A Roman Adventure (Part Two)

My friend Cindy M. and I packed a lot of sights into our week in Rome, but none was more interesting than our visit to see the Necropolis (city of the dead), an ancient burial ground that lies deep beneath Vatican City.

To see this amazing archeological site, you must request special permission from the *Scavi* (excavations office) and book tickets by emailing them at least three months in advance, since only a few timed visits are allowed each day.

With great anticipation, we began our tour by descending a steep flight of steps with ten other folks and slipping through sliding glass doors into the damp, dimly lit, and uneven corridors leading to the crypts, ending up beneath the Basilica at the believed tomb of St. Peter himself. Talk about walking through time!

We ended this fascinating day by strolling the narrow cobblestoned lanes of Trastevere, on the west bank of the Tiber River. The area is filled with pubs and excellent restaurants, so choosing one shouldn't have been too hard, right?

Several waiters leaned from their doorways in a pool of warm orange light, beckoning us to enter, while delicious smells, boisterous conversations, and the clatter of dishes tempted us to step inside ivy-covered restaurants that oozed charm. But we didn't stop. We were looking for just the right place.

More and more people, mainly locals, began to fill the streets, all with single-minded purpose. They were headed for the tastiest places to eat.

Did we follow them? No.

Did we consider the locals would know the best place to go? No.

Were we a couple of dummies? Yes.

We saw people lining up for many of the dining establishments, but we didn't want to stand in line. Lining up is for chumps.

Finally, we spied a forlorn little restaurant around the corner from the crowds. A place as empty as the mausoleums we had visited that afternoon. A place where the entire staff stood beseechingly at the door, their dark eyes pleading us to step through the portal and seat ourselves.

So, we did.

Hurriedly, they swarmed us, gratitude written across their faces. A menu was thrust into our cold hands, and the worst wine I've ever tasted was glugged into my glass. We were smothered with uncomfortable attention.

Once our meals were delivered (with much bowing and scraping), the waitress hovered over the back of Cindy's chair, vulture-like, eyeing every morsel she lifted to her lips. Another waiter swept the floor beside us, taking sideways glances at our plates. Still another cleaned and re-cleaned every table within a ten-foot radius, watching our faces anxiously.

This scrutiny was off-putting, but it wasn't the worst part. The food was, in a word, *terrible*—flabby pasta, a few crumbles of mystery meat, and a heavy-handed plying of the oil jug. *Blech.*

Courageously, we labored through a small portion of it, then paid and dashed to freedom. *No wonder they had looked so pleading.*

Keep in mind, bad restaurants can be found anywhere, but local people know the best places to eat. Follow them, even if it means waiting in line.

So, there you go: a couple of tips, complete with colorful examples, brought to you straight from the streets of Rome.

Hmm—perhaps I should have been a travel writer?

Move over, Rick Steves!

Beaver Tales

"Some of my best friends have been beavers."—
Helen Row Toews

If you're now shaking your head in bewilderment at this bizarre revelation, I'm not surprised. It's a strange admission to make, but I've always had quite a soft spot for the furry rodent.

As a kid, I'd perch on a huge log that had fallen across one end of a pond west of our house, and I'd read or write in the good company of a few ducks, a muskrat or two, and the hidden beavers.

Leaning my back against a gnarled old poplar, I'd dangle my feet over the water and while away the hours. The beavers didn't come out during daylight hours, but I knew they were there, waiting for twilight. I watched them go about their work a lot back then, and they grew used to me, after a fashion, only casting me the occasional mistrustful glance as they came ashore for food.

My warm, fuzzy feelings toward them have been sorely tried, however. During the last fifteen years, we've seen several young beavers move into the neighborhood, operating under some crazed notion they can turn the shallow creek bed beside my home into a thriving water hole, where a happy family could be raised twenty feet from my back door.

I would have no objection to their close proximity, except that they plug the culverts and build complicated dams, causing the creek to back up and flood. Two years in a row, the water rose so high that the bridge we built to access the rest of the farmyard parted company from its moorings and floated off downstream.

Crossing over it required a long pole to steer (vaguely reminiscent of Venetian gondolas, but not really), rubber boots, and a bunch of dumb luck. It was a bit unsettling to clamber onto a bridge that immediately drifted away from shore and toward the open sea. (Slight exaggeration, for effect.)

In order to reach the other side, it was necessary to take a hard run at the platform, leap aboard, and shoot across, balancing as though riding the waves on a Californian surfboard. While fun for kids and for those of us with an adventurous spirit, the laughs wore thin—fast.

Another year, when my daughter, Rebecca, still lived at home, the busy rodents again made terrible pests of themselves. In order to construct bigger and better dams, they began selecting choice young saplings from my yard. How maddening is that? Constructing a dam at the edge of my property was bad enough, but to use my own trees for the job—inexcusable!

One night, Rebecca lay in bed listening to frogs croaking outside her window. It was a warm summer evening, and a fresh breeze wafted across her pillow as she slowly drifted off to sleep. Suddenly, a strange noise broke her slumber.

It sounded for all the world like gnawing. Leaping up, she peered out her window and into the darkness, straining her eyes to see what was happening on the lawn. It was close, just a few yards away, and Rebecca listened as a resounding crash filled the air.

"Oh no, you don't!" she muttered grimly, as she slid on her boots and stole out the side door. Moonlight spilled through the branches of a poplar tree close to the creek, and once her eyes adjusted, she could see the toothy culprit dragging his spoils toward the pond. Sprinting across the lawn, she grabbed the opposite end of the poplar, fumbling for something sturdy to hang on to in the thin branches at the top.

The critter had to have known she was there, but he wasn't about to give up his prize. Throwing a shoulder under it, claws gripping the soft ground, he bore down, and slowly began making headway. What a sight it must have been: a resolute, buck-toothed beaver straining with all his might at one end of the tree, and an equally determined girl in a flowery flannel nightgown and Wellingtons digging in on the other!

Resting peacefully in my bed at the opposite end of the house, I had no idea my young daughter was battling a brawny beaver in the backyard. Ultimately, Rebecca realized a dead tree wasn't going to do anyone much good – apart from the beaver, so she let go. Busily, he pulled it to the water's edge and dove in, pulling my tree behind him.

Yes, we've had some scuffles with them here on the farm, but, what the heck: I still like the plucky little varmints.

Bon Appetit!

Over an Easter break, my dear friend Susan and I skipped the country for greener pastures. They truly were greener, too, since snow fell unceasingly on the Prairies throughout our time away.

We flew to Paris initially and ended our trip in Amsterdam, where flowers bloomed in colorful profusion, trees hung heavy with blossoms, and fattening treats called our names. "Helene et Suzanne," they trilled in beautiful French accents, enticing us from the window of each boulangerie.

We told ourselves that with all the walking we did, the calories from such rich pastries and delicious breads would soon be worn off. Clearly, we are easily duped. In any case, it was a fabulous trip, and I thought I might share a little of it with you.

Over the course of a few days, we were whisked to all the highlights of Paris by the Métro (subway): we stood before the famous Eiffel Tower, gazed upon the Arc de Triomphe, strolled the Champs-Élysées, and wandered within the great Notre Dame cathedral.

We were impressed by Sainte-Chapelle, a stunning Gothic chapel of stained glass that was built quickly and completed in 1248 to safely store precious Christian relics belonging to King Louis IX. As shafts of light filtered through the countless panes of colored glass, a stillness fell upon the crowd, who stood with awed faces upturned in the rosy glow.

Another interesting place we visited was a renowned teahouse called Angelina, located near the Tuileries Garden. It was my birthday, and I wished to celebrate by sampling its legendary hot chocolate. It's a luxurious location that has been frequented by many well-known Parisians, including the iconic designer Coco Chanel.

Naturally, what's good enough for Coco is good enough for me, so after a heavy lunch elsewhere, we stood patiently in a que and then were ushered within its portals.

The immaculate waiter, who bade us follow him, paced majestically through opulent surroundings to our table, and I immediately felt uncomfortably aware of my old scuffed shoes and a nasty stain on my jacket from an earlier indulgence. As well, it was cold in Paris, and I had taken to wearing almost every item of clothing I possessed.

Sadly, this created a personal look not unlike a stuffed pork sausage, as I shuffled past tables of slender, well-dressed customers. Sigh. It was busy, and space was limited, but I managed to squeeze between several tables and drop awkwardly into an ornate chair. Tables are arranged much closer together in France.

After peeling off several layers (and almost taking out the eye of my neighbor), I looked happily about me.

"Isn't it beautiful?" Susan whispered with hushed

decorum, as we stared at the mosaic floors, lavish, gold-plated mirrors, pale-mint walls, and soft lighting from crystal chandeliers.

We turned our attention to the menus, delivered by another smart-looking waiter who was too well-mannered to gape at the bulky items of clothing I had piled behind me, or at my hair that rose toward the roof in a frenzy of static electricity after dragging two sweaters over my head. Susan wisely opted for a simple croissant and coffee. I scanned the dessert listings.

Snapping the menu shut, I smiled across at my chum, "How big can a cup of cocoa be? I'm going to have pastry, too. After all, it's my birthday."

Moments later, the waiter glided soundlessly to our table and began to dispense numerous dishes. I sat for a moment, overwhelmed by the huge pitcher of rich, brown liquid, pot of whipped cream, and slab of decadent strawberry dessert now in front of me.

What had I done?

Hoisting the pitcher with some difficulty, I moved to pour the liquid into the supplied cup, but it wouldn't budge!

My friend and I exchanged shocked glances as I held it upside down. Nothing. This was no ordinary cocoa, but a vast allotment of molten chocolate. With the help of a spoon and a lot of loud scraping, it consented to flow like thick, cooling lava into my cup.

A glint of laughter lurked in Susan's eyes as she recalled our recent meal elsewhere.

It took every bit of fortitude I possessed to grimly work the whole business down my throat that day, but at the price I paid for those delicacies, I wasn't going to leave a crumb.

Coco would, doubtlessly, have asked to be moved to another table, far from the country bumpkin who had lumbered into such a fine establishment.

She would probably have been appalled at such inappropriate attire and certainly at my lack of self-restraint.

Nonetheless, apart from struggling to later fasten my coat, and some noticeable difficulty drawing breath—or, in fact, speaking—I enjoyed an unforgettable experience with a wonderful friend in Paris, who barely mocked me at all.

Vive la France.

Gesundheit!

As I stare with puffy, sleepless eyes at my computer screen tonight, I'm happy I can lurk in the shadows, quietly being sick at home. If you've ever come down with an illness—God forbid diarrhea—on holiday, I'm sure you'll agree.

One cold March, my seventeen-year-old daughter, Aliyah, and I visited family in England, ending with a three-night stay in Edinburgh, Scotland.

Sadly, we both came down with a horrible cold that laid us flat. Also sadly, and in keeping with my miserly ways, I'd booked a cheap hotel with the offhanded remark, "As long as it's clean, who cares?"

Except that I should have cared, since it was tortuous to lie on what felt like a slab of three-quarter-inch plywood and to feverishly shiver beneath blankets thin enough to spit through (to quote my father), while wind, sufficient to sail the Spanish Armada, whistled under the door.

By the second day of suffering, we needed medicine and food, because the vending machine was running low.

Don't get me wrong: I can easily make a meal from chocolate, but two days' worth was pushing even my limit.

I croaked at a maid from our doorway to ask about the

nearest grocery store, and whether or not I could walk there in my weakened condition.

"Och, it's nae trouble at awe. Joost a wee ten minute. Ye cannae miss it," she said, pointing toward the street.

I thanked the woman kindly for her barely intelligible directions and collapsed back on the bed. *Ten minutes, hey?* I suited up and wheezed downstairs.

After half an hour of trudging, I leaned heavily on a lamppost and subsided into wracking coughs.

Where the heck was this place? Pushing myself upright, I asked directions of a woman walking her dog, but with a withering look of disgust, she tugged at his leash and hurried past to avoid contamination. I drew a shallow breath and stumbled on.

Here's what I know to be true: when in a foreign country, whether sick or not, the place you're looking for is *never* just a ten-minute walk, and you *always* miss it.

I was also deathly ill this past summer in Spain. Cringing under the sheets with a terrible headache, I sent my long-suffering husband, Tom, out to buy pain relievers on the *Gran Via* (the busiest shopping street in Madrid) in peak tourist season, during a gay pride parade, in sweltering plus 42°C heat.

After two hours, I started wondering if I'd ever see the man again. Tom is directionally challenged at the best of times, and this might well have been his end.

As I lay moaning in the darkness of our hotel room, a wet rag I'd found hanging over the bidet draped across my forehead while I listened to Tom's choice of entertainment (a John Wayne Civil War movie dubbed into Spanish— not something I'd watch even in my mother tongue), I considered his chances of survival.

I imagined his corpse, crumpled in some nameless back alley, clutching a bottle of medication in his lifeless hand—a poor lost man, overcome by heat and crowds.

Or perhaps he'd been swept into the parade as he innocently crossed a street and was now marching, with bewildered, faltering steps, on to Barcelona, banner held high.

In any case, he made it back safely, and all was well.

It's great to be at home when you're ill.

Great, Just Great!

Isn't it great to get your hands back into the earth and start planting again? Whether you have fields, flower boxes, or gardens to tend, it does a heart good to break into the rich brown soil after such a long winter.

Of course, it's not so great to get your hands into the earth if a cat has recently squatted there, or a dog has deposited some toothsome treat beneath the crust.

We don't have outside cats, but I know how unpleasant that situation can be, and as for the dog problem, sit back and let me tell you about it.

Upon exiting my house this past week, I noticed my flower beds had been ripped up. Fresh dirt had been dug and piled right where I'd planted the precious tulip bulbs I'd faithfully carried home from Holland several years ago. *Blast!*

As is often the way, I first accused my long-suffering husband.

"Tom, have you been scrounging around in my flower bed?" I asked irritably, but his denial was truthful enough.

My eyes narrowed upon Chili, the family dog and bane of my existence. Well, not really the bane, but a few of her escapades are hard to forget, like the day she methodically chewed a gaping hole into the drywall beside her bed, or the afternoon she made a leisurely deposit the size of a small badger on my newly purchased area rug.

She looked back at me, tail wagging, the picture of innocence and good humor. I found my trowel and bent to investigate. It didn't take much effort to reveal the shinbone of a recently deceased cow hidden in a shallow grave among the mangled remains of my tulips.

Great.

Then, as I was loosening the dirt in a large tub by the house, my trowel hit upon another obstacle. I'd been transplanting petunias and hadn't bothered with wearing my gloves. Oh, how I wish I had. Fishing about in the soft earth, I grabbed what felt like an article of clothing. Granted, it was furry…

"*Argh!*" I screeched, tossing the flattened remains of a partially chewed gopher high into the air.

Double great.

Chili and my brother's dog, Gibson, often get into scrapes together. Several times we've had to go load them up and bring them home from one place or another.

This winter, as I was returning to the farm in my school bus after work, I glanced toward the house of a new neighbor in our area. I observed Chili and Gibson frolicking about in the field beside the neighbor's garage.

Drat. Those dogs are up to it again. Angrily, I laid on the horn, knowing that if Chili saw the bus she'd run for home.

Honk, honk, honk! I leaned on it loud and long, but the dogs paid not the slightest attention. They gambled about in the snow, bowling over each another and moving onto the front lawn to continue their fun.

With increasing annoyance, I yanked the vehicle to the side of the road and slammed open my window.

"YOU BLOODY DOGS GET HOME," I hollered at the top of my lungs. They paused to gaze at me with only mild interest.

"GET HOME!" I screamed, punctuating my sentence with further honking.

It was then that the homeowner strode into view, lifting his arms in a time-honored gesture that clearly said, "What in the hell do you think you're doing?"

And, it was then that I realized the dogs weren't ours. The new neighbors also owned two mutts almost identical to ours.

Triple great.

Never a Dull Moment

Working with kids is never dull. Nope, it's filled with an endless variety of situations, problems, and questions asked by fertile minds. Those minds may not always be on schoolwork, or on what people are saying to them, but they're undoubtedly active. Let's look at a couple of examples, shall we? Of course, names have been changed to protect the innocent.

I was working in a classroom of first grade students this past spring, where the teacher was educating her class on various forms of precipitation. It was a good lesson—well prepared, delivered interestingly enough—had they all, in fact, been listening.

However, it had been a long afternoon for one little chap in particular. And his attention wavered between a bit of old chewed-up eraser and a mangled paperclip he'd procured from the floor near his desk (almost anything can be turned into a toy with enough imagination).

These items danced across Oliver's desk in happy delight, until the teacher instructed him to put them away. With the audible sigh of a condemned man, he shoved them out of sight and turned a small bored face to the speaker, resigned to his fate.

The teacher had moved on to the topic of hail and sleet by this time and was drawing the lesson to a close. She began to involve the children in a short question period in order to see if they'd retained the information.

"Can anyone tell me what type of precipitation we might receive on a warm summer day?" she inquired brightly, smiling at the kids to encourage a response—any response. Several arms finally went up, and the correct answer was found.

Meanwhile, Oliver slumped in his chair, a toe scraping along the floor to create a small, but gratifying noise. His fingers twitched under the radar of the teacher's eye, as he acted out some tragic life-and-death scene on his lap (at times, one must rely on the simplest of props for entertainment). It was just as one of the two main players in this pathos was toppling off a cliff to certain doom that the teacher called his name.

"Oliver! Are you listening? What have you learned about snow?"

Oliver jerked to attention. His hands fell to his sides, and his feet grew quiet as he faced the front with strained features and blank eyes.

"Snow?" he repeated slowly in an effort to play for time. Tilting his head to one side, he drummed a finger on his forehead, as he cast vainly about for any possible shred of information on snow he might have available.

"I KNOW THIS," he hollered, coming bolt upright out of his chair with relief and excitement. "If it's yellow, don't eat it!"

While driving the bus after school one day, I heard an exchange between a young brother and sister. It wasn't difficult to hear, actually, because toward the end, it was delivered at the top of the sister's lungs. In fact, it reached such a high decibel that I was forced to intervene, lest the racket continue on forever, causing my brains to implode. It all began with a simple request from a little girl to her sibling, who sat two seats behind her.

"Joey?" she called sweetly, "I want to tell you something."

Joey, a boy well-accustomed to these appeals, said nothing and continued his lively discussion with a friend across the aisle.

"Joey?" her voice grew louder and more insistent. She turned, craning her neck out into the aisle, and, after a deep cleansing breath, commenced a routine well-known to the participants.

"Joey. Joey. Joey," she yelled, each time raising her voice in intensity, each time like a nail being driven into my noggin.

"JOEY. JOEY. JOEY," the spaces between each word were shorter now, much like the rapid fire of a machine gun shot from the back window of a getaway car to warn off the coppers.

Naturally, everyone *except* Joey had paused and had turned toward the tiny girl who continued her staccato bursts, "JOEY. JOEY. JOEY."

"Stop!" I hollered, my eyeballs bugging out of my skull. "What is it that you have to tell him? Is it really that important?"

"Yes," she said simply, her big blue eyes searching mine, blonde curls bobbing as she nodded vigorously. "It's *very* important."

"All right, Joey," I said briskly, looking back at him in my mirror. "Listen up. Your sister has something important to tell you."

She swiveled toward him, as every eye and ear on the bus tuned in to witness this marvelous piece of information about to be delivered.

Her moment had arrived. A self-satisfied smile played on her lips, and a distinctly smug expression washed over her face as she glanced around at Joey, fluttering her eyelashes. "I got candy today. And you didn't. So, NAH-NAH."

Yes, life is full and rich when you work with kids.

The Magic of Spring

This past weekend, my grandson, Kayden, arrived for another memorable visit. Together, we ate things that weren't good for us, frolicked with newborn calves, and waded through every mud puddle we could find. We even had a snowball fight; although, I have to say that Kayden would have made a sneaky sort of gunslinger.

Back in the old west, on episodes of *Gunsmoke*, Marshal Matt Dillon would have never shot a man in the back, or gunned down unsuspecting folks from the safety of a building, no matter what kind of low-down, dirty, rotten varmints they were. And he would most certainly not have taken such potshots at his *own* grandmother. However, Kayden paid for these poorly thought-out schemes eventually. When you get older, you're expected to revert back to childhood—right?

There's something about springtime that frees your soul and makes you feel young again—or youngish, anyway. When the sun warms your face, and a warm breeze clears the winter frost from your brain, it's hard not to feel reborn right along with the rest of the Earth. I think we who are fortunate enough to live in the country have, perhaps, a special kinship with this rebirth—a closeness to the land and its inhabitants. Maybe this sounds a bit fanciful, but I have a story to back up my theory.

It happened quite a few years ago, on a frosty April

night. My three children were concerned about their mare, Tina, who was heavily in foal.

"Maybe tonight," Dad had said, stroking a hand along the mare's swollen side. We'd gathered to assess her condition, as she stood placidly in a snug shed at one end of the field. Everyone agreed there was a contemplative look in her eyes, as well as a few other, more telling signs.

Dad turned, noticing the worry on each small face, and hastened to reassure. "She's had plenty of foals in her day. She'll be fine."

Later that night, I woke in the inky stillness of my bedroom and sat bolt upright to check the clock. It was 3:00 a.m. *Why had I awakened?* Something was wrong.

I pulled a coat over my pyjamas and stole silently out of the house. High overhead, the moon cast her silvery glow across the path before me, as I hurriedly crunched through the glittering grass, watching clouds of my breath puff away on the still night air.

Unexpectedly, a loud moaning noise shattered the silence of the night, becoming louder and more tortured with every passing second. I broke into a run. Over the fence I flew and dashed into the pasture to see Tina lying flat upon the frozen earth and a large, white, struggling mass behind her. It was the foal making the horrible gasping sound! Fully encased in the amniotic sac, it couldn't breathe, and as I got closer, it ceased its feeble struggles and was still.

"Tina!" I yelled. Startled out of her exhaustion by my

sudden appearance, she snorted and lunged to her feet. As she did so, the sac was torn away from the tiny creature within, and Tina wheeled around to begin nuzzling him.

After a few tense moments, I saw the foal lift a shaky head, and I dropped to the ground, my heart racing, to watch the age-old bonding take place.

While I don't profess to be any more in tune with nature than the next guy, I'll always be grateful I was wakened that night.

Green Thumbs

I really appreciate houseplants, especially throughout the winter months, when the thought of spring becomes a foolish little dream. I'm not as good at growing them as some people, but I try. Sadly, there is one variety of plant I love, but have never been able to keep alive—a Boston fern.

I have a friend who likes them, too, and several years ago, she had a dandy. During each visit to her home, I'd see it sitting proudly in the front window, its emerald fronds sweeping her hardwood floor.

"His name is Klaus," she'd said fondly, giving him a loving little spritz of water. After a few months, I asked for the secret to her success.

Her eyes darted guiltily away. "To be honest, this is the fifth Klaus I've had," she sighed deeply. "I can't grow them, either."

While I'm not sure how the sad scenario played out for her, I'd get one from a greenhouse and tend to it lovingly, allowing myself bright hopes for its future. Then a leaf would flutter to the floor, and I'd know it was all over. Despite my best efforts, it soon became the spiny, lifeless husk I knew so well.

There was one time, however, when I was able to grow a wonderfully fertile specimen. It was in a cool place with indirect light. The soil was kept moist, and every month I gave it a good soaking with pure rainwater. I fertilized sparingly and frequently misted.

By golly, it flourished!

Then one hot summer day, I stood at the window keeping an eye on my children who were playing outside. A smile crossed my lips as my eldest son, Chris, came into view, leading his younger siblings on some wild adventure of destruction and mayhem, as was his custom. Turning, I glanced at my healthy fern and moved to fetch the water bottle. In this heat, it surely needed a drink.

Grabbing the mister from beneath the sink, I applied the water generously, shining beads of moisture lingering on each lush green leaf. But, wait! What was that smell? Why was the nose-wrinkling scent of Javex suddenly floating on the afternoon air? I lifted the bottle and took a whiff. Bleach?

"CHRISTOPHER!" I hollered out the door, as I charged past with the fern. Plunking the poor thing in the tub, I started the shower. Maybe the poisonous effects could be rinsed away?

Meanwhile, Chris appeared behind me with a carefully constructed "look of innocence." He didn't know why he'd been summoned, but applying his look of innocence was the safest bet until he figured it out.

"Why have I just misted my favorite plant with bleach?" I ground out between clenched teeth.

Jauntily, he began answering back, "I don't know. Why have y—" until I fixed him with a glare, known to my kids as "the look of death." He fell silent and took a sudden interest in his shoes. "Well, it might be because I put some in there to kill ants on the sidewalk," he finally mumbled.

"WHAT?" I roared, and he scampered out the door, wisely not returning till suppertime, when I'd cooled down.

In any case, the fern died, and that was the last one I grew. Just didn't have the heart for it anymore. Give me a geranium or a nice succulent, even a hoya, and I'm good to go.

Just keep those poor bloody ferns in Boston.

It Could Be Worse

"Rain again. In seventy years of farming, I've never seeded the fields so late!" Dad leaned on the sink, gazing out the kitchen window, where streams of water had begun their descent for yet another day. He turned away shaking his head, but catching my eye, a smile slowly widened under his bushy, gray mustache.

"Ah, well," he said with his customary optimism. "It could be worse."

I confess that there are times when people with so much bloody, bright-eyed cheerfulness are very annoying to those of us looking forward to a day spent in a morose downward spiral of self-pity. However, as I've always found, father knows best. It's healthiest, for mind and body, to focus on the silver lining—hard as it may be to find.

From a duck's point of view, the weather's great. I see them happily frolicking in sloughs and ditches each day, as I rumble down country roads in my school bus. Carefree and light of heart, they paddle in large clusters by the road to mull over the day's events, or assemble gossiping in ditches.

"Have you seen Bert and Harriet's new nest? I mean, seriously—who uses mud and sticks anymore?"

Serenely, they paddle about in water mere inches from my tires, calling eagerly to friends, "Sally, Maurice. Get the kids and come on in, the water's fine."

Naturally, just as I pull abreast of the laughing crowd, Sally turns. Spotting the enormous yellow monster thundering down upon them (or so it must seem to a duck), she leaps into the air, quacking loudly, "Alert, alert! Everyone out of the pool!"

Then, flapping wildly, with crazed indecision, everyone rises awkwardly into the air, veering off in the safest possible direction—directly in front of the school bus.

Dumb ducks.

Mud hens are worse. They often collect in small groups at the water's edge in the gravel alongside the road, muttering among themselves as I roar past in the school bus. I advanced upon a few of them the other day as they stood, huddled together arguing.

"Look, we need to get to the other side, okay," said Maxwell Mud Duck, self-appointed leader of the group.

He strutted importantly around the doubtful throng. "I say we act now. And flying is out of the question. I've given this a lot of thought, and our best course of action is to run out like a pack of lunatics in front of that bus."

His wife piped up from the sidelines in loud accusatory tones, "Cousin Frankie followed you on one of your harebrained schemes last week, and we all know how that ended!" The ducks all turned to stare at several mangled black feathers protruding from the mud.

All right. I admit that wasn't the best plan, but I tell you, I know what I'm doing now." Maxwell's voice rang with conviction, as he glared with irritation at his foolish wife. The troop surged around him with renewed confidence (mud ducks aren't all that bright).

They paused a second more, waiting for just the right moment to fling themselves into oncoming traffic. Heads bobbing, eyes vacant and trusting, they milled around their fearless leader.

"This is it!" he cried, suddenly lunging onto the road. Without hesitation, they rushed forward as one, necks craning, little legs propelling them like pistons as they ran pell-mell under my wheels—to certain death.

Oh, don't worry. I didn't actually hit the silly creatures. I was expecting their heedless dash across the road and had slowed. But if I hadn't…

As we can see, this wet weather suits some of us just fine. And if it doesn't, sadly, there isn't much we can do about it, anyway, so you might just as well sit back, read the newspaper, and have another cup of coffee.

It could always be worse. Be thankful you aren't a duck.

Two Wheels that Move the Soul

My brother recently purchased a handsome Harley-Davidson. It's his pride and joy. He keeps it safely tucked away under lock and key until he needs to slip away from everyday toil and send the cares and worries of life tumbling into the breeze that whistles past his ears.

I understand.

There are few things better than swinging onto a motorbike and hitting the open road on a hot summer afternoon.

Back in the day, I used to ride one myself. Surprised? Well, it's quite true. There was a 250 Suzuki trail bike that took me on many grand adventures. And then, for a period of time, I owned a street bike.

A black leather jacket and a sparkly red, full-face helmet were part of my constant attire, complete with a black visor that, when opened for conversation's sake, looked for all the world as though I had survived, somewhat like Darth Vader, inside a hermetically sealed microwave oven.

It was I who taught my oldest son, Chris, to ride a motorbike, which may or may not have been a good thing, but it's too late to take back now.

A couple of summers ago, I was quietly tending flower

beds when I heard what sounded like the angry whine of a low-flying jet. I looked up, shading my eyes against the sun. Some lunatic was doing a wheelie across the entire length of the field across from our home! Then, this crazy person roared down into the ditch and ramped off the other side, flying high in the air—and into our driveway.

Was it Evel Knievel?

Speechless, I stood holding my trowel as the bike skidded sideways to a halt in a shower of gravel, and Chris hopped to the ground, beaming happily.

"Isn't it great?" he cried, brushing a few impaled bugs from his brow. "It's a CRF450 Honda dirt bike. I'd like you to take it for a spin and try it out," he finished proudly, as the rest of the family emerged hesitantly from the house.

I edged toward the gleaming machine. *Good grief, I hadn't ridden a bike in twenty years, let alone a monstrous one like this. Was it even possible—or wise?*

Would I careen headlong into the ditch and require several sturdy men wielding an acetylene torch and wire cutters to extricate my mangled body from a barbed-wire fence?

Would I end my days in horrible disfigurement after grinding face-first along our gravel road in a heap of twisted metal, or be forced to ride on into infinity, because my feet couldn't reach the ground to slow down and turn the blasted thing around?

The engine rumbled loudly as I thought. *No, I couldn't refuse and disappoint my son when he so clearly had faith in me. Plus, there was a certain amount of pride involved.*

I had to do it.

Strapping on Chris' helmet, I grimly accepted a boost in order to get on the thing, and eventually managed to growl off down the driveway, mouthing a silent prayer.

In the end, however, it all went quite well. It felt good to speed through the gears and feel the wind rush past my face, as it had so many years ago.

I like riding bikes.

Maybe I should get one again—if only I still had my flashy red helmet.

First Jobs

Hurrying into a popular housewares shop recently to return some drapes, I was reminded of what it was like to start a new job. The very young girl behind the counter looked at me with a concerned frown as I skipped past the empty area where folks queue up to pay and headed straight for her.

"Excuse me!" she called with the air of one who had been taught correct procedure with *no* exceptions. "You can't enter there. You'll have to wait your turn in the line." I opened my mouth to argue that there wasn't one, then closed it again, and did as she asked.

"Next, please," she beckoned with a bright smile, as, moments later, I reached the front.

We've all been there, I suppose. When I was fresh out of high school, my first job was at a public library. I was young, nervous, and entirely lacking in the social graces. (Unsurprisingly, time has worked its magic, and now I'm *old*, nervous, and entirely lacking in the social graces.) But back to my story.

For some unknown reason, the mayor of our city and several notable officials invited our library staff to join them for a prestigious dinner.

I sat quietly, keeping my usual low profile, as speeches

were made and congratulations given. Afterward, a plate was clunked onto the table in front of me by one of the stony-faced waiters who glided soundlessly about the room, the embodiment of decorum and fine manners.

I glanced at my food. *Horrors!*

I had been allotted, among other things, a large clump of raw cauliflower. *What was I supposed to do with that?* I couldn't pick it up or break it apart with my fingers, and I couldn't spear it and gnaw the thing in midair. It didn't occur to me to leave it alone on my plate. I'd been brought up to eat what I was given. (Thanks, Dad.)

Grabbing my utensils, I began to saw discreetly. Progress was slow but steady until my knife slipped, and the white lump hurtled into the air like an errant snowball and bounded across the floor to rest along the main passage to the kitchen.

Crud!

Now what? Ignore it? Pretend it belonged to someone else?

"Can you believe that?" I could have said disgustedly to my well-dressed neighbor. "Some people have such dreadful table manners!" and I'd dab my mouth with the corner of a linen napkin and look all superior and stuff.

Or should I lunge to my feet and collect it?

I imagined how I could stand to face the head table and with a courteous inclination of my head say, "A thousand pardons, distinguished administrators, but I appear to have dropped my cruciferous vegetable."

It was while I was frantically thinking, that a waitress burst from the kitchen door with a heavily laden tray. The scene played out before me in terrible slow motion, as she stumbled over the cauliflower, plunged one hand into a nearby potted plant to catch herself, and flung the tray and its contents high into the air.

I shrank into a miserable huddle and had nightmares for weeks, all ending the same way—me crouching miserably in a dank, dimly lit prison cell, while stylish accusers, each sporting the head of a cauliflower, advanced upon my cowering form.

"It's hers," they'd scream, jabbing long, razor-sharp forks at my head.

So, yeah, first jobs can be traumatic.

Cut the kids some slack.

Travel is a Great Teacher

Exercise sessions on my treadmill have lately become opportunities to visit far off lands on YouTube. These videos I watch, taken by someone on a drive or walk through the cities and countryside of Europe, have given me the ability to escape each morning on an exotic trip: rambling through the Cotswolds of England, where time has stood still for three hundred years, and clusters of honey-colored, stone cottages nestle between the softly rolling hills.

Or I go strolling through *les ancient villages Français* and down medieval cobblestone lanes, as the cicadas sing their timeless song in the nearby plane trees. Time passes quickly as I imagine I am there, rather than trudging endlessly on my machine, going nowhere fast.

Only last summer we visited several of these places, and not a day goes by that I don't think of them. Travel is my passion.

Inevitably, though, I've made some blunders.

Mostly ones that cause us to walk farther, take a wrong bus to who knows where, or suffer some sort of acute embarrassment. However, I always learn from my mistakes, and that's what counts.

In Spain last summer, I realized that extra care should

be taken when checking dates and times of departure and arrival. Sadly, I had us exit our hotel early Tuesday morning in order to catch a flight that didn't leave till Wednesday. My teenage daughter, Aliyah, was up at five (no mean feat) to be ready in time. We packed, tidied the room, and marched downstairs with heavy bags, only to find we were a day premature.

Hubby, Tom, was cheerful and philosophical about it as we returned to our room, while Aliyah leveled a baleful glare at me for much of that day.

I've learned that sometimes spending a little extra cash for a slightly upscale excursion can be money well spent, as noted during the blazing July heat of Madrid, when we slid back and forth in an unpleasant pool of our own sweat on the cheap plastic seats of a bargain bus tour.

I've discovered that saving fifteen dollars by gobbling cheap sandwiches on the street, near St. Paul's Cathedral in London, is no savings if your husband spies a top-end menswear shop across the road and nips over to spend the next hour buying eighty-dollar shoes.

I gathered where an old, well-known expletive must have come from. Painstakingly, in 40°C heat, we ascended the narrow streets of Toledo, the former capital of Spain. From around a hidden curve ahead, a van transporting several swarthy men and a swaying load of cured hams hurtled toward us. We flattened ourselves against a nearby wall, and as the tires crunched only inches past our toes, we closed our eyes and hoped for the best.

"HOLY TOLEDO!" Tom yelled with a broad grin, once it had passed.

Tom found out that adding a fake accent to the English words we speak, according to each country and language spoken, was not always appropriate or appreciated when he altered the standard terminology for what he wanted and ordered an "*El Whoppo*" in a Spanish Burger King.

I learned that dragging a protesting daughter on to a random bus in Edinburgh, simply because we were tired, and it was "going our way," was not the smartest choice, when we ended up dockside on the shores of the North Sea.

My reassurance, "Calm down. It has to turn around and go back sometime," fell on angry ears, because, of course, it didn't.

Ah well, as long as we can learn from our mistakes, right? And I've made enough of 'em to fill a book.

But I keep on tryin'.

What's Sense Got to Do With It?

"I like collecting sticks," the little boy responded, after turning his head to one side and tapping a thoughtful finger on his chin. The children in my school had been asked what their favorite outdoor activity was, and we'd received the usual answers: "riding bikes" and "playing with friends" and "visiting the playground." This was unexpected.

"Sticks, hey?" I asked.

"Yeah," he replied carelessly, "but not so much anymore, since Mom told me I had too many damned sticks. She says the backyard is full of 'em." He leaned closer and lowered his voice confidingly: "I got a lot of sticks."

I hid my smile, but it caused me to think later about my own youthful outdoor activities. I used to like cycling. Lately, I've taken it up again in order to stave off obesity during this 2020 COVID-19 pandemic.

It's been good. My daughter Aliyah and I pedal down our road in the crisp evening air, discussing everything from Shakespeare to Charolais cattle. (Okay, we don't really discuss cows. I threw that in to please my father, the cattleman.)

On our latest excursion, I told her of a bike ride, taken years ago with my brother, Bill. He's five years younger than me, yet we were inseparable then. Naturally, as the oldest,

I took the lead when it came to important decisions. Stuff like: whether to swing on the corral gates (after we'd been expressly forbidden), climb on the stack of square hay bales (also prohibited), or cross the creek on a raft made from an elderly tire tube and a hunk of rotting plywood. Often—all right, usually—these choices ended in disaster.

But, I digress. One afternoon, when I was about twelve, we found ourselves pedaling far from home. Dad was fixing a fence in a far pasture, and we meant to surprise him. Refreshments, consisting of a thermos of coffee and a roughly made peanut-butter-and-honey sandwich, jangled in my metal bike basket.

Laughing, we rounded the bend beside a thick poplar bluff and gazed down the road ahead.

YIKES!

Trotting toward us was an insignificant animal with a powerful presence.

A skunk.

He stopped, we stopped—the whole world stopped—as we eyed one another, not ten feet apart.

From the corner of my mouth I hissed, "When I give the word, drop your bike and run."

Likewise, Bill addressed me sideways, his lips barely moving, "Wouldn't it make more sense to ride the…"

"NOW," I hollered. My bicycle clattered to the turf, and I sprinted away. Still doubting this wisdom was Bill, running close behind.

Perhaps similarly questioning my sanity was the skunk, who also took his leave, but with far less drama.
"I still think we shoulda ridden our bikes home," Bill grumbled from a nearby hill, as we paused to pant. "And what about Dad's lunch?"

It was a reasonable question, but one that I wasn't prepared to entertain until that evening, when our irritated father returned from the field.

"It's bad enough you kids can't take care of your things at home, but now I find your bicycles tossed into the middle of a road half a mile away! What are you playing at?" Aliyah snickered as I relayed the tale. "You weren't a very sensible kid were you?" she said.

It was more of a statement than a question and sadly was true, but when you're young, what's sense got to do with it?

Congratulations!

It was a busy and emotional time this past week, as our youngest daughter, Aliyah, graduated from Lloydminster's Comprehensive High School. We're very proud of her, as I know all other parents are equally proud of their sons and daughters. Each graduate has worked hard to reach this pinnacle of achievement.

The school staff, parent committee, and volunteers also worked hard to create special graduation events, under difficult circumstances (COVID-19), so that the kids would have memories to treasure for a lifetime. We're all very grateful to them.

It was an exciting time to be sure, and although our son, Justin, oldest daughter, Rebecca, and I were a snug fit in our small car's back seat, we happily watched as Aliyah received her diploma and participated in the "Grand March."

Granted, once Justin, who had been waiting outside his home to be picked up for this event, clambered into the car, the atmosphere in our vehicle became somewhat suffocating, due to his absent-minded indulgence of a clump of chives that grows near his front step.

Who does that?

Whatever would possess someone to chomp down on a fistful of green onions prior to sitting thigh-to-thigh with family members forced to share the same air with you for the better part of three hours?

Although they weren't even there, I blame my Manitoba uncles for Justin's lapse in judgment. They taught my children from an early age to enjoy such atrocities as peanut-butter- and-onion sandwiches.

Anyway, not even onions, or the residual breath thereof, could dampen our spirits on this momentous day.

Until we got home, that was. Aliyah's sparkly dress was hung back in its protective bag, Rebecca left to do her laundry, Justin went home to brush his teeth (I hope), my husband began trimming his toenails, and I dealt with a nasty mealybug infestation.

Talk about a rude jolt back to reality.

I didn't even know several of my plants were infected with the dastardly insect until a friend texted to inform me that the hoya I'd cheerfully given her for her birthday was diseased. She warned me to check the other plants.

Have you ever laid eyes on a mealybug? They are horrid. It took me three hours with dish soap, Q-tips, and a washcloth to clean them off my plants, and each day begins with a frantic search through the foliage for more.

For several nights thereafter, the bloody things even crept through my dreams. I couldn't get a wink of sleep as I wielded an enormous Q-tip dipped in coffee (don't ask) to battle a group of enormous mealybugs that had slinked through the flower bed, leaving their foul, white residue on my petunias, then moved on to suck the life out of my leafy greens.

To be honest, I now have mealybugs on the brain and see them everywhere I look! I even caught myself closely examining a plastic plant in Walmart for the sinister creatures. I have to admit that some form of therapeutic intervention may be needed in order to put this whole unpleasant interlude behind me.

In any case, I must come back to the original point, before things take another ugly turn and I get started on my wood tick rant. Onions and mealybugs are quite enough for one day.

Congratulations to all graduates everywhere! You deserve much praise.

Real Riches

Is it just me, or have you noticed an increase in commercials promoting wealth management companies lately? Wait. It's probably me. I haven't really noticed them, since I own nothing to speak of, and have no discernible wealth to manage.

Considering the last advert I saw, catering to clients ranging from extremely affluent to ultra-high-net-worth individuals (otherwise known as "stinkin' rich"), it's no wonder I didn't pay attention. Now, if there was advertising designed to reach folks labeled as "impoverished" or "dirt poor" or "penniless," I'd be apt to listen up.

Money's always been an issue for me. When my children were little, we looked forward to summer holidays in Manitoba with family, but gas was expensive. In order to finance this trip, we'd spend evenings and weekends picking bottles for the necessary cash. It wasn't so bad. With a ball cap pulled low over my eyes and sporting an old discarded jacket of Dad's, I'd slop through ditches in a pair of rubber boots, my identity hidden.

However, my kids were not as enthusiastic, and they often suffered the profound sort of embarrassment as can only be felt by young teens. Who wants to be defined as a family that pilfers through the refuse of society for five-cent pop bottles?

One day, as we skulked through the overgrown grass of a ditch near their school, my eldest son, Chris, who had been lagging behind, stared at an approaching car, stiffened to attention, then threw himself prostrate into the weeds.

"Get down, you fools!" he hollered. "That's the principal's car. HIDE!"

But it was too late. The sleek gray Buick slowed as it neared our location and crunched to a halt in the gravel close by. Rolling down a window, the man leaned across his console and addressed me with concern as I stood in a patch of thistles, holding a grimy box of Pilsner beer.

"Excuse me. I'm wondering if your son Chris is all right. He's lying in the grass about fifty feet back, clutching an empty bottle of vodka."

"Ha ha, yes. He's fine," I hastened to assure the man, as a sudden image of myself cowering before the court on charges of child endangerment crept through my mind. Making matters worse, I caught sight of my eleven-year-old daughter, Rebecca, who was standing behind me with a can of Labatt's Blue beer in her hand.

"He's just resting," I assured the man once more.

He smiled, clearly unconvinced. Reluctantly, he motored off, watching us closely in his rear view mirror.

Another time, a carload of older teenagers roared past me on the road. I could hear one yell, "Here, lady," as they screeched to a stop, lowered the window, and tossed an empty to the curb.

There's nothing that says "bag lady" quite as well as when a woman, attired in a ragged mackinaw grubby from spending the bulk of her day in a ditch, eagerly scuttles across the road in rubber boots to pick up a discarded pop can and shove it in her grocery sack. Sigh.

Yes, I'm no stranger to money troubles, but consider all the wonderful things I have: beloved family and friends, the symphony of frogs I hear through my bedroom window late at night, the scent of sheets having blown dry in a Canadian Prairies breeze on my bed, and the joy of unearthing the first crocuses of spring beneath the prairie wool grass near my home.

I'm rich after all.

Dream or Nightmare?

Ever had a dream where you're out in public, perhaps shopping in a busy mall, delivering an impassioned speech, or mingling with roughly one hundred of your peers at a 40th high-school reunion (my actual nightmare), then glancing down, suddenly realize you're wearing nothing but your pajamas, or worse yet, are naked? I have. And what if it happened to you in real life? Well, not the naked part, but the pajamas thing?

These days, many people leave the house to run errands in fuzzy flannel pants, but it still remains an uncomfortable vision for me. That's why I was a fool to exit my home last week in some crazy yet comfy pj's I'd purchased for my youngest daughter, Aliyah, some years ago.

I'd been home sick all day with a cold. Curled up on the sofa under three blankets, I drank honey-lemon tea and watched my favorite daytime television program, the *Marilyn Denis Show* through bleary eyes. My friend Kim had driven the bus for me that morning, but couldn't later on. Knowing this sad fact, I still somehow managed to fall into a fitful slumber.

Suddenly, I reared upright and consulted the clock.

How long had I been sleeping? Good grief—there was only ten minutes till school let out! I lunged for the door, snatching sunglasses and keys as I dragged my wheezing carcass to the bus. It was only once reaching the road I realized I was not properly dressed.

Peachy.

I consoled myself with the fact that no one would see me. I keep a low profile at the best of times, but behind my shades and sitting low in my seat, who would ever know?

Of course, I forgot that nothing gets past little girls, and one paused beside me to remark, "What a strange outfit you have on, Mrs. Toews. Is that a tail?"

"Ha ha. Don't be ridiculous," I croaked, my face flooding with color as I hurriedly stuffed the thing out of sight. "Now, hurry along and take your seat."

I breathed a sigh of relief as we pulled away from the school, but when we arrived at the home of a sweet little kindergarten girl, I could see I was now beaten. Her mother was walking out to meet her.

It has been my experience that small children take a considerable amount of time to prepare for any type of departure. Especially if you'd like them to hasten. Calmly, the child rose and peered out the window to assure herself we were in the correct yard. Then she began the labor-intensive application of her jacket. After zipping up, she reached leisurely for her backpack, pulled it across her tiny shoulders, and adjusted the straps.

Meanwhile, her mom had reached the door of my bus. I opened it with a sigh, and she looked in. Her jaw fell slack, eyes widening with questions yet unspoken as she took it all in.

I was slumped on the seat in a fluffy, head-to-toe, fuchsia-and-black leopard-print "onesie." The hood, complete with long cat ears and googly eyes, hung like a cape around my shoulders, and a lengthy, spotted tail brushed the floor beneath my seat. I grinned stupidly at the woman and between fits of coughing tried to babble out some sort of believable explanation.

The woman made an effort to nod understandingly—as though it were commonplace for her child to be ferried about the countryside in a government-issued vehicle driven by a large pink cat—smiled wanly, and with several backward glances over her shoulder, hustled her child off to the safety of their home.

Okay, so maybe it's not quite of nightmarish quality, but the whole awkward, unpleasant scene could certainly have featured in one heck of a bad dream.

Making Memories

Sharing laughter around a campfire with family and friends is only one of the many activities that make summer on the Prairies great. Recently, we did just this when family from England visited us during their first trip to Canada.

Hoping to make their time in Canada memorable, we decided to take them to the Thunderchild First Nation Pow Wow and Handgame Championships. What a fabulous celebration of tradition it was! The singing, dancing, and regalia were fantastic, and the people were welcoming. Bannock burgers were enjoyed, vibrant images of the dancers were snapped, and everyone took home memories of this piece of Canadian heritage—a truly inspiring event. I think we all should attend a powwow to better understand traditional Indigenous life and culture.

On other days of the visit, we went for walks, drove an all-wheel-drive truck across the farm to check cattle, and kept a sharp eye peeled for wildlife. We fed them Saskatoon pie, homegrown beef, as well as other Canadian specialties, and ended most nights seated around my brother Bill and sister-in-law Linda's firepit, gazing at the stars.

On a side note, a mouse darted into the house during this momentous family visit. After vacuuming my ceiling (long story, but suffice it to say we have a wood stove, and smoke makes things messy), weeding the garden, tidying the house, and painting a few gates (to spruce things up for their arrival), it was seriously disheartening to spy all three cats hunkered near the door, peering hopefully under my washing machine.

Drat! It would be hard to maintain my facade of quiet Canadian grace while rushing about the house whacking mice with a mop. Also, the presence of vermin does not lend a ringing endorsement of one's cleanliness.

However, in all the flurry that morning, the rodent was forgotten, and when we returned that night, the cats were nonchalant about the whole affair. They sprawled on the sofa, the picture of contentment and ease.

Perhaps I'd imagined the whole thing?

After a wonderful four days, with hugs and promises to visit soon, we waved goodbye to our relatives and trudged back to regular life and work, which, for my husband, Tom, meant delivering diesel and gas to fuel stations throughout our area.

It was a hot day, and when he appeared in the kitchen beside me late that afternoon, I wrinkled my nose. There was a sudden whiff of something vile. I looked around the room suspiciously and opened a few cupboard doors to take a deep breath within.

Tom said he'd shower and help search it out. Interestingly enough, the stench left with him. While not wishing to outright tell the man he stunk, twenty years of marriage allow a certain level of forthrightness.

"Hey," I said when he returned. "That stench was you."

We narrowed it down to his feet and then shook each of his boots at the door. Sure enough, out tumbled a bedraggled, decidedly flattened mouse.

Yikes!

The cats often drop toys into our shoes, but this took a cute game to a whole new level.

Amid peals of laughter, my daughter Aliyah and I recounted the day's events:

- Tom sliding clean white socks into oversized steel-toed boots and ignoring a slight obstruction at the toe—dead mouse.

- Tom treading heavily throughout a 30°C, eleven-hour day, feet sweltering—dead mouse.

- Tom motoring off to Edmonton, Alberta, in a huge truck, a rodent stowaway resting lightly on his toes—dead mouse.

Poor man.

And—of course—poor mouse.

But memories galore.

A Country Wave

I'd like to draw your attention to a phenomenon seen only in Canada's rural areas: the country wave.

I refer, of course, to the silent salute shared between the occupants of two vehicles passing, like ships in the night, along a gravel road.

Allow me to explain. We country folk wave at all those we pass. They may be neighbors, or we may never have laid eyes on them before. It makes no matter. It's a gesture of camaraderie and acceptance that can't be found anywhere else but along a country road in our great land.

This friendly gesture is not to be confused with the courtesy wave, which is a brief signal of gratitude to a fellow motorist who has shown respect on the road, or the apology wave given after some inconsiderate maneuver, like cutting off another vehicle. The latter is usually accompanied by a guilty grin, a slight shrug, or a decided averting of the eyes.

Certainly, it's not the flirtatious wave, randomly wiggling all fingers at shoulder level, used almost exclusively by women with effective results.

Nor is it the regal wave, popularized by Queen Elizabeth, in which the hand is cupped and moved slowly to and fro at a steady, measured pace. This signifies good breeding and restraint. You'll never catch the queen flapping her arm like some nut, in order to seize the attention of a friend across the street.

We've all seen or been a part of the clan brotherhood wave between truck drivers and motorcyclists. This isn't what I'm speaking of, either, although it's getting closer. This wave is exclusive. Only those belonging to either group are included in the signal.

It's more a sign of professional respect between those who understand the inherent difficulties of a job, or a collective love for a mode of transportation representing freedom and nonconformity.

No, the country wave can be described in this short talc. When I was a child, our family often went for a Sunday drive. We'd ramble through the Saskatchewan countryside wherever the wind blew us, enjoying a rippling field of grain or lush green pastures dotted with cattle.

Unfailingly, my father would lift a hand of acknowledgment to each passing motorist, as they did in turn. Wondering how the heck my father could know everyone in a one-hundred-mile radius, I recall questioning him on it one afternoon, miles from home.

"No, I don't know those people," he responded, smiling down at me from beneath his worn brown Stetson. "It's just what country folks do."

I don't suppose he'd given it much thought, as may be the case with us all. However, if you consider it, this simple expression of friendship assures us that we do not stand alone. For better or worse, we're all in this life together and share in the common bonds of community and solidarity found in folks living close to the earth.

It's a silent communication that guarantees help, should the need arise. People who live in the country pull together in tough times and rejoice together in good.

All tied up in a little wave.

Meeting the Folks

A while back, our eighteen-year-old daughter, Aliyah, summoned up her courage and announced she had a boyfriend. Naturally, we were expecting this to happen one day, maybe somewhere in the distant future, when she turned thirty-five. I guess we're guilty of voicing that age-old parental lament when children grow up and leave home all too quickly.

Sigh.

In any case, Aliyah was a little nervous to broach the news to us, then nervous all over again when the day came to introduce him to us in person. However, we like Arron, and all is well.

It's a difficult business to introduce a boyfriend or girlfriend to family members, and I'm sure Aliyah also felt a bit awkward the first time she met Arron's parents. I know I did when I met my future in-laws.

Unfortunately, I was a bit of a nut.

I mean, yes, I was, and still am, a simple country girl from the sticks, but there was a period of time in my life when my nickname was "Wheels"—I rode a motorbike, wore a black leather jacket, and had purple hair.

Let's face it: none of these qualities makes a good first

impression on parents.

Maybe if I'd driven sedately up the driveway in a nondescript sedan, or caught the Greyhound bus into town and walked primly to their door, or even had my father drop me off in his grain truck loaded with seed oats, I'd have had a chance.

But no, I had to rumble into their driveway slouched low over the handlebars of a street bike with muffler issues.

Even after that, if I'd have worn a heavy woolen toque to cover my outrageously colored head of hair, or knotted an old scarf of my mother's tightly around my throat and complained of laryngitis, or pulled one of Dad's "Charolais Beef Is Best" caps low over my ears, I could have eased into their midst a little better.

But no, I dragged a helmet from my head and slung it over one arm as I waltzed up the sidewalk with straggly, grape-colored locks blowing in the breeze.

It was during the "punk" era, what can I say?

If I'd have thought for two minutes, I could have slipped on some sensible footwear and a cashmere cardigan with lace trim, or popped on a brightly patterned muumuu worn by moms in the '70s, or even donned some filthy calving overalls Dad kept in the barn. Anything would've been better.

But no, I clomped into the room wearing enormous boots and a leather jacket that sported a scrape up one arm, where I'd skidded on my bike down a gravel road.

Thankfully, the whole Wheels nickname wasn't acknowledged. It wasn't like I had it emblazoned across my back in flames or anything, so I was safe there—for now. But, these things do have a nasty way of getting found out.

Foolishly, none of this concerned me until I strode into the kitchen, where my boyfriend's parents were visiting with his sister and her children. They'd heard me arrive (the whole neighborhood had) and were now waiting, with trepidation.

There was a stunned silence as I entered the room, and the innocent youngsters who had been playing happily near the door took one horrified look and flung themselves under the dinner table, cowering in fear.

Despite entreaties to "Come out and meet the nice biker lady," and offers of warm cookies and milk, they would not emerge. Nothing could persuade them to stand in the presence of so dreadful an apparition, and they clung to the table legs with tiny ashen faces.

That was my first clue that things were gonna be awkward.

Fortunately, they were wonderful people who accepted me despite their first impressions. But yeah, meeting the folks can be a tough gig.

I should know.

My Sincerest Apologies

Before our family headed out on a European adventure this past summer, my young daughter of sixteen worked hard to learn a few civil words in the language of each country we would visit. She took great pains to drill me on them, too.

When I least expected it, she would pop up to pose a pertinent question.

"Mom, do you remember how to say you're sorry in Spanish?" she'd ask over the broccoli salad.

Or, as I was flying out the door to work, she would ask, "How do you admit guilt in German?" There was no escaping her, even while showering, as she even queried through a crack at the bathroom door, "Can you properly ask forgiveness in French?"

"Sheesh. What's with all the apologies?" I finally asked, an edge of irritation in my voice.

Turns out that she expected me, quite rightly, I suppose, to mess up royally each time I set foot on foreign soil. Presumably, her feelings of shame, as I regularly make a fool of myself locally, were nothing compared to the concerns she had of global embarrassment.

This apparent lack of faith eventually got me worried,

and I threw myself even harder into the online French classes I was taking. However, I must take umbrage with a few of the more impractical French phrases I learned.

The likelihood of a situation arising in which I would feel compelled to reveal that "My mouse does not have a brother" seems wildly implausible. In fact, it was unlikely I would ever engage a French citizen in conversation at all, let alone broach the sensitive subject of domesticated mice, particularly my own. And any discussion of their kin, or lack thereof, seemed, to me, ludicrous in the extreme.

Now, here is an all-time favorite phrase: "You have a fat pig." Oh my, the times I've used this line in an effort to win friends and influence people.

Never.

On holidays abroad, the average person rarely spends time touring hog barns, while the idea I might be placed in a position to assess anyone's weighty swine seems remote at best.

In the interest of world peace, it's probably an ill-advised idea to strut around announcing to French people their pigs are fat — even if it's true.

Let's examine another good phrase I learned online. "I am going to eat an entire chicken." When does the average person feel the need to say this, I ask you? Certainly, there are no restaurants, to my knowledge, that serve whole roasted chickens to their patrons.

I can only assume, therefore, that this line is meant to be inserted into polite conversation. Perhaps, while strolling through a French market, I might pause near the fresh poultry counter and lean confidingly toward an elderly man, waiting for some duck legs to be bagged.

"*Psst!* Hey, bud," I'd hiss from the corner of my mouth, with a furtive glance down aisles to either side of me. "Later on, I'm gonna eat an entire chicken."

Now, if the online course had concluded this lesson by teaching me how to say, "How much is bail?" or "These handcuffs are chaffing," I would have paid closer attention. Naturally, the prescribed French phrases I learned aren't all that ridiculous. These are just a few of my favorites.

And despite my daughter's fears, I managed to muddle my way through our journey without an ugly international incident.

We saw some wonderful sights and met some lovely people. Of course, there was that one nasty episode involving a little old lady, several ripe melons, and a dog — I still feel bad about that one.

Désolé, madame!

Birthday Bash!

My stepdaughter, Nicci, recently celebrated a milestone birthday. I'm sure it was a day filled with mixed emotions, as all such events are. Since we live on the far west side of Saskatchewan, right against the Alberta border, we weren't able to spend it with her, since she lives in Manitoba, but her father called, and I wrote several long messages. Of course, she knew what sort of wishes to expect from me on this pivotal day.

Many years earlier, this same (at the time) lovely twenty-something woman had told me about her recent visit to an eating establishment run entirely by "old women." She'd been shocked that such a restaurant, which professed to cater to a young, vibrant clientele, would actually hire these aging ladies.

"How could women of such advanced years keep up the pace," she had asked in wonderment? "What a distasteful statement it made. Were the faces of these 'old women' representative of the depths to which this previously thriving business had sunk?" Nicci shook her head in disbelief.

I began to envision the scene as she continued painting the rich colors of her experience at the popular Italian eatery. I saw white-haired grannies in pastel cardigans, sensible footwear (with added arch supports), and thick, brown foundation hose, scuffling painfully between tables with their arthritic hips.

A few pushed walkers in front of them, which made carrying trays of food tricky, and often they'd pause to sit a while on the little built-in seat, before laboring to their feet with a groan and continuing on.

People loudly bellowed their orders at the ancient waitresses, who, leaning ever closer, cupped blue-veined hands behind their ears in an effort to hear properly, then asked customers to repeat it three more times, anyway, just to be sure.

The staircase had been torn out, and an Acorn Stairlift had been installed to allow ease of movement between the dining floor and the kitchen, but the food was still cold by the time it reached the patrons, due to the understandable limitations of rheumatism, bad circulation, and problematic knee-replacement surgeries.

All the chairs were crushed velvet and crowned with embroidered doilies, while plastic roses decorated the pale Formica tabletops. Along one side, a sizable mahogany record player stacked with Lawrence Welk LPs played softly, and in the corner, several of the staff, on their break, played a slow game of shuffleboard.

The hostess loudly ordered people to, "Mind they didn't track in mud," at the door, and then insisted they, "Eat all their peas," as she rolled past later in her motorized wheelchair to seat new arrivals.

Cat fur lingered on everything, and a faint, musty smell

of mothballs wafted throughout the room, despite the restaurants specialty dishes of pizza and pasta extraordinaire.

I could see it all in my mind's eye and clucked disapprovingly with Nicci, as we discussed how standards had been lowered in this once-youthful establishment.

"Incredible," I observed in amazement. "What age do you suppose these old women were?"

"Oh, let's see," she said reflectively. "I'd say they were at least forty." Nicci raised her horrified eyes to mine. "Can you believe it?"

"WHAT!" I cried, with the sense of pure outrage only a woman in her forties could summon.

And so, dearest Nicci, it is with the deepest love and admiration for the gorgeous woman you are, that I say to you, "Happy fortieth birthday! It really isn't all that old."

Business Blunders

Running a home-based business is a tough job. Of course, sales and marketing seem to come naturally to some folks. They're the sort of people who could sell water to a drowning man, and I'm the sort who couldn't sell water to a man whose house was on fire. This truth was recently evidenced at a local farmers' market, where I sat with books for sale.

To pass the time, I decided to search for my website on the Internet and found, for some obscure reason, that a company had analyzed its value. After tallying the profits and running the numbers, it turns out I have an estimated net worth of—hang on to your hat—$8.95. And I apparently rake in a whopping fifteen cents per day.

Step aside, Bill Gates.

That's when book sales are brisk, obviously, so I can't expect that kind of big money to roll in every day.

When I was younger, I tried my hand at several home-based businesses, and not one of them was successful. The first was for a popular cosmetics company. I like makeup well enough; I've even been accused of single-handedly increasing the sale of ruby-red lipstick worldwide, but liking it and selling it are totally different beasts.

Mostly, I urged people to save their money rather than

spend it, which is a bit counterproductive. Plus, there was the whole demonstration component, where I was expected to apply makeup on naive participants. Sadly, after a party that was later referred to as the "clown-face incident," women got a bit reluctant. (News travels fast on the home-party pipeline.)

Then came the crazy day I was talked into selling lingerie by a woman promising easy money and a lifetime supply of fuzzy pants. Whatever made me think I could do that?

Showing large groups of women flannel pyjamas, cozy fleece, or cotton nighties was one thing, but when I found out I'd have to personally fit them with heavy-duty, corrective brassieres, I was done. This introvert collected her personal space, yanked on some steel-toed work boots, and learned to drive a truck.

A sucker for punishment, my one last attempt was to sell vitamins and healthy cosmetics, so good for you that they were actually edible. Of course, that wasn't recommended, but still. These were worthy products to be sure, but again, selling them demanded a skill set I didn't possess. Nonetheless, I tried my best, held a few parties, and filled a few orders.

However ill-advised, my husband supported me in this venture and wished me well, as he grabbed his lunch and dashed from the house. He was late for work that day.

Later that morning, I stood at a customer's door, happily handing over her order. Unfortunately, all thanks died on her lips as she slowly pulled a loosely wrapped bologna sandwich from the bag and squinted at it in the sunlight.

I stammered out an apology and made my escape, fully realizing that this was not the worst of it. Right about now, my husband would be taking a well-earned break. He would fling himself onto a hard bench in the doghouse (he worked on an oil rig at the time), open his lunch bag, and stare in horror at two pink lipsticks, a jar of cold cream, and a lovely palette of earth-toned eyeshadow.

Edible? I think not.

And that was where I threw in the towel. To all of you who run a home-based business, you have earned my respect.

An Uncultured Lout

It was as I visited the exhibition of a world-renowned artist this summer that my anecdote begins. I found the show highly entertaining, but not quite in the way the artist might have hoped. It did, however, teach me something quite profound about myself, and here it is: I am an uncultured lout.

Allow me to explain.

Entering the first of many silent, softly lit chambers at this exposition, I passed stiff, uniformed guards keeping a sharp eye peeled for troublemakers, then I paused inside the doorway for a moment, to drink it all in.

I'd been excited to lay eyes on the incomparable art within these protected vaults and gazed about eagerly, surprised to see that the first piece featured a urinal as its focal point.

This innocent bathroom accessory was attached to the wall, then, for no apparent reason, had been mercilessly bashed to bits with a rock. (I know this, because the rock in question was included as part of the exhibit.)

Among the shattered remains of the poor porcelain fixture was a short length of plastic pipe, arranged strategically on the floor next to the rock.

I stepped back to fully appreciate this object, tilting my head, and squinting thoughtfully in the hope some purpose for it all might manifest itself.

Nope.

Moving on, I was treated to the sight of a brutally beaten refrigerator. It looked as though it had been hit repeatedly with a garden spade. Thankfully, not three feet away was an explanatory video, filmed as the actual beating took place. It clearly depicted the battery of this blameless icebox, again by means of a large rock hurled from the shadows.

Two inoffensive television sets also squatted nearby, smashed beyond repair. Their guts spilled forth unpleasantly onto the floor, and other rocks appeared boldly among said rubble.

This is art?

Further along, another secured room housed a montage of black-and-white etchings. Evidently, the artist had concluded his tableau using the humble stone as a medium by which to "create," and now, with that out of his system, had moved into the mixed media of paper, pen, and pencil.

In the first scene, the revered artiste appeared to be undergoing some desperate inner turmoil, as he scrawled back and forth across the paper in bold, harsh lines. Others illustrated a more perpendicular motif, perhaps signifying joy or—all right, cut the malarkey!

They were a collection of reckless scratchings: six hens, a

handful of oats and some dirt could have created the same thing in five minutes. (This is where the uncultured lout part comes in.)

Sadly, I am but a simple country lass, uneducated in the ways of true art—because I didn't get it.

I do, however, have a theory, if you'll bear with me. It can be summed up in the story of *The Emperor's New Clothes*, by Hans Christian Andersen. An emperor was duped by two scoundrels into believing that the clothes they had made for him (which did not exist) were only visible to people of great refinement and intelligence. Those who were uncivilized or foolish saw nothing. Since no one wanted to stand out from the crowd and be thought of as a fool, all the townsfolk pretended to see the emperor's beautiful clothing as he paraded about town in his underpants.

It is my uneducated belief that we all behave in this way at times; we pretend to admire or agree with something outlandish (not always art) simply in order to fit in with the masses. It's daunting sometimes to have an opinion that is contrary to popular belief, for fear of looking foolish in the eyes of the multitude.

This leads me back to my earlier statement of personal loutishness. I was unable to appreciate these celebrated works of art that have been lauded by art lovers around the world and must, therefore, conclude I lack sophistication and refinement.

However, consider the aforementioned story of the emperor. Perhaps I'm wrong, but maybe it deserves some thought.

The Young and the Foolish

My daughter Aliyah pulled on her motorcycle helmet and tightened the strap under her chin, as I pelted her with instructions.

"Now, don't go fast and watch for uneven ground. Keep both hands on the controls at all times and scan ahead for potential problems. Lean against turns to offset tipping, stay off main roads, and…"

"Yes, yes, mother. I've got it," she answered irritably, rolling her eyes. "I'll be very careful."

As she manoeuvered out of the yard on an all-terrain vehicle, or quad as they are often called here, I heaved a worried sigh. She was a responsible seventeen-year-old girl. I had to lighten up. How the heck had my parents done it? I don't remember them plaguing me with undue regulations and restrictions.

How did they live through my adolescence without suffering from the high blood pressure and anxiety attacks I seemed to experience now as a parent? I slumped on the front steps, head in hands, reliving just one of the foolish incidents of my past.

I must have been about eighteen and in possession of both a 250 Suzuki trail bike and a casual disregard for safety. My friend Lori was spending this night with me on the farm, and between us we had hatched an evil scheme.

Well—it wasn't so much evil as it was just darn dumb.
Once my trusting parents had gone to sleep for the night, Lori and I crept soundlessly outside. In the moon's silvery glow, we found my old bike leaned against the pump house and painstakingly pushed it down the road about a quarter mile, since it made too much noise to start it in the yard. (We certainly didn't want to alert the folks.)

This bike had issues. As well as lacking a muffler, it was short taillights, turn signals, mirrors, and a kickstand; although, it did sport a fairly decent headlamp. In any case, my erstwhile companion stood to one side as I jumped on the kick-start, and the engine throbbed to life.

We grinned at each other in the wavering beam of a flashlight we'd brought from the house.

Success!

With the heady excitement of teenagers up to no good, we hopped aboard and roared down quiet backroads to visit another friend in Lloydminster. Lori had no spot to rest her feet for this trip, but no matter. She shared my footrest, as we zoomed through the midnight air.

When it was time to head home, I decided (with all the wisdom of a rock) that it would be quicker to go down the highway.

"But we have no taillights," Lori wisely pointed out. "How will drivers behind us know we're there?"

"That's easy," I yelled confidently, as we motored out onto the Yellowhead Highway. "Flip the flashlight on and hold it over your shoulder. People will see that, for sure."

And so, she did.

We rumbled home without a care in the world. Two silly girls on a wretched old motorbike, in the middle of the night, one holding a flashlight behind her back, as they streaked along a busy Canadian highway.

Next morning, Dad eyed us intently over his oatmeal, as we dragged ourselves into the kitchen.

Dryly he remarked, "You might want to push that bike a little farther down the road next time, Helen. It's pretty bloody loud."

However did my parents put up with me?

Necessary Evils / Finding Love

As I sat in a waiting room after having driven a friend to her colonoscopy appointment, I considered the whole subject of unpleasant medical exams—hers, in particular, and mine by extension. Happily, for me, I was able to wait outside with a newspaper as she was wheeled away on a gurney.

Until the moment she walked into the hospital and stood at the admissions desk, I wasn't sure if she would even go through with it, but swilling back a gallon of grape-flavored laxative isn't something you do on a whim—escape was futile.

Turning to me as we scuffled off down the hallway she had hissed, "They asked for photo ID. Can you believe it? Who in their right mind would want to fraudulently attend someone else's colonoscopy appointment? They'd have to be crazy!"

I giggled uncomfortably, feeling her pain. I've undergone various tests, too. In fact, as you may well expect, I have a tale to tell along this theme. (Insert disclaimer here.)

In order to set the scene, you must know that I was single prior to this procedure, and friends had invited me to a dine-and-dance. It had been a lovely evening. We'd eaten well, cavorted about the dance floor, and met some interesting people, one of whom was a strikingly handsome fellow with aristocratic bearing, impeccable style, and perhaps a poor sense of humor, but I could've worked around that.

Fast forward a week. I entered the Manitoba hospital, where I lived at the time, and was handed disposable blue booties and the usual backless gown. Yay.

Once attired in these offensive garments, the nurse led me along a cheerless passage and through swinging doors to where a cold steel slab awaited my presence. Double yay.

With his back to us, the physician busily clattered instruments onto a tray and instructed the nurse to have me lie down. Then whirling about with a grim smile, he began to introduce himself. His voice trailed into nothingness. We had met before: he was the man from the party—and I was having a barium enema.

Yikes!

My face must have registered the horror I was feeling, but apart from that first jolt of recognition, he quickly smoothed his features into a mask-like neutrality.

"Roll over, please," he stated calmly, "and extend your posterior. This may hurt a little. Try to relax."

"*RELAX?*" a voice screamed in my head. *Was he for real?* The whole episode had quickly taken on a nightmarish quality not unlike an Alfred Hitchcock movie.

Relax? Really?

What kind of nut could feel at ease when a handsome, eligible man sees you, not only attired in paper slippers and sackcloth, but is required by his profession to run a tube up your butt and introduce a foreign substance into your cramping bowels before snapping photographic evidence of the event for later consideration?

People have managed to form lasting relationships in the midst of some rather strange circumstances, but let's be honest: once an enema has been administered, it's pretty much game over.

We parted ways without further eye contact or comment and have never spoken again. Medical procedures are important, but as precursors to lasting relationships—not so much.

Hoarding

It's been a bit tricky to come up with fresh ideas for columns during this COVID-19 business. Not much happens when you spend the majority of your day hunched over a computer, or crawling through the garden, weeding carrots.

With that in mind, perhaps you'll forgive me when I tell you that this week's thoughts were precipitated by that well-known show *Hoarders,* which can be seen on the A&E network. It features a team of experts who have limited time to help people deal with extreme hoarding issues.

I can't claim any moral high ground here and announce that I've never watched the program, because I've seen a few. I suppose we have a morbid fascination with the program, because, by contrast, we can all feel better about our own ghastly mess.

One such episode follows a man who took up residence in a garden shed after being evicted from his home by roughly 2,500 rats. Can you believe that?

Although I haven't seen the episode, I can almost picture this unfortunate fellow clutching the only two things the rats would let him take: a change of socks and a faded photo of dear old Mom, as, against his will, he is carried prostrate from the premises on the shoulders of several thousand vermin and tossed to the curb.

Then, I envision the assembled rodents dusting themselves off, marching back inside, and slamming the door. Sort of like when the family feline threw Fred Flintstone out of his own house and locked the door behind him.

While it could not be said that my childhood home was spotless, it was reasonably tidy when my brother and I were kids, so when Mom and Dad decided to clear the attic of everything that had accumulated there for the past 40 years and dragged it all downstairs to be sorted, things got messy.

Old cream cans, trunks of clothes, and winter boots that hadn't seen feet for two decades were deposited in the kitchen. Framed paintings of long since passed English relatives, boxes of chipped dishes, and a battered tricycle littered the living room.

As more and more junk filled these rooms, Dad began piling it high, being careful to leave a narrow trail open to facilitate movement from one room to the other, as well as to important places, like the potty and the refrigerator. Brother Bill and I quite enjoyed this strange system of trails through the rubbish that had appeared in our otherwise empty living space, and we happily played games among it—until someone knocked at the door.

We stopped in stricken silence.

Who could it be?

Perhaps it was a carload of vacationers from the nearby

town of Marsden needing directions, or a Fuller Brush salesman who would get no farther than the doorstep?

But, no.

Our eyes widened with horror as the local Anglican Church minister paced majestically (or so it seemed) into our midst and stood gazing about himself in open-mouthed amazement. Acting as though nothing was amiss, my mother invited the man to sit down a spell and have a cup of tea.

Thus, the reverend and his somber black trench coat trailed through the confusing maze, and he seated himself gingerly on a chair my father hastily swept clean of assorted junk. He denied thirst when offered a beverage, and conversation was strained as he peered at us over several dead plants, a stiffened pair of cowhide chaps from 1897, and a rusty enamel chamber pot that perched precariously on our coffee table.

"There's just one thing," I said, as the door closed behind the man, and we all breathed a sigh of relief. "Did you guys look at the pamphlet he left behind?" I held it on high for everyone to lean in and read the title of next week's sermon.

Cleanliness is Next to Godliness it proclaimed with confidence.

"We're in trouble," Bill muttered.

Stick 'Em Up!

While driving with Dad to attend the seventieth wedding anniversary of precious family members Maurice and Shirley Anderson, in Ardrossan, Alberta this weekend, I saw two funny bumper stickers.

The first was plastered to the back end of a dilapidated old car at the edge of a road: *PLEASE DON'T HIT ME! I'm not 100% sure about my coverage.*

Cute, right?

The next one passed us on Highway 16. The sticker was a takeoff on those yellow diamond-shaped signs new parents put in the back window of their car. The ones that urgently proclaim, *BABY ON BOARD!*

I've always wondered how those things worked. Are they some sort of lucky charm, warding off bad drivers and unforeseen accidents?

Also, if the presence of babies requires added caution, what about children past the age of three? Or adults? Do they cease to matter?

You don't see signs such as *DIFFICULT TEEN ABOARD* or *AGING COLUMNIST WITHIN.* Although, I guess you could, but it'd be a warning for reasons other than safety.

Enough of my foolish ramblings. The sign I saw on the passing car announced, *ADULTS ON BOARD! We want to live, too!*

Funny stuff.

I've also had a bit of personal experience with stickers. At my recent high-school reunion, I was given a large one and asked to print my name in big letters, so people could tell who in the world I was after all these years. Thank goodness for them, too.

One woman rushed to my side soon after I entered the building, wrapped me in a bear hug, and exclaimed how good it was to be together again. She spoke knowledgeably of school days, class antics, and treasured memories. I laughed delightedly, returned the hug, and agreed that it had been far too long, all the while thinking, *Who the heck is this person?*

Leaning my head sideways in a careless gesture of bonhomie, I frantically read her name tag. In truth, that still didn't help me remember who she was, but at least I was able to address the woman by name. *Whew.*

Then there was the time I helped out at a kids' camp. There were more than one hundred kids to feed, so the organizers decided to run them through a chute, like a herd of cattle.

Well, that may be my own interpretation of the events, based on life as a cattleman's daughter, but it was true. At one end of the line, where I worked, people issued stickers.

On them we printed each kid's name in capital letters, and a sentence indicating what condiments they wished to have smeared on a hotdog they'd receive further along in the line. I had a sticker, too, just to show the kids how it was done.

After a wild couple of hours, I pushed the hair away from my exhausted face, got in my car, and drove to the grocery store. Oddly, as I trudged through fresh produce, I noticed people staring, smiling, and even pointing at me. *What was up?* I thought.

Then, as I reached for some radishes, a white-haired woman leaned toward me, winked, and said, "Hotdogs are thataway, deary."

With a sigh of painful recollection, I looked down at the message emblazoned across my chest: *MY NAME IS HELEN, AND I'D LIKE A HOTDOG WITH MUSTARD AND KETCHUP.*

Great, I thought.

Made a fool of myself yet again.

What's new?

The Truth Will Set You Free

Why is it that when human beings are accused, blamed, or questioned—either rightly or wrongly—our first inclination is to immediately deny responsibility? It's a reflex action, I suppose. Of course, this is never truer than when we're young, when rebuttals are spat from the mouth as easily as brussel sprouts.

"Who left these crayons on the table?" was the simple question recently posed to a class of first grade students by their long-suffering teacher. It was, in fact, a non-threatening question delivered by a mild-mannered, smiling woman of kindness, but it might as well have been rapped out by the grand inquisitor just before he signaled a firing squad to take careful aim.

An immediate chorus of denial rang out. Earnest faces, with wide guiltless eyes, claimed their innocence, cited their whereabouts at the time of the crime (far, far away), and denied any involvement whatsoever.

Nonetheless, although not themselves on the scene, they were, surprisingly, able to see and know who *had* been there, and easily identified their friends as possible perpetrators of the deed. As is the case in many crimes, the culprit was never found.

Interestingly, along this same theme, that very night I found a pair of small red gloves on my school bus, forgotten and alone. The next morning, in an attempt to locate the owner, I held them aloft as each child climbed aboard, but everyone denied ever having seen them before.

How odd, I thought. I protested the point after the last child was seated, and everyone turned a bored face to listen—sort of.

"These gloves have to belong to someone," I said encouragingly. "I'm not accusing you of mitten neglect: there'll be no court case; the police will not be called; there is no blame to be laid. I simply wish to give you your gloves." I searched each set of vacant eyes, feeling exasperated as tiny shoulders shrugged.

This isn't the first time I've seen such a phenomenon. It's played out every, single, solitary day at school.

"Is this your book?" I ask. "No." (Their name is written inside.)

"Did you spill this juice?" I ask. "No." (They're holding a dripping apple beverage.)

"Is that your candy wrapper on the floor?" I ask. "No." (They're eating candy.)

Once the children had exited the bus, I was forced to consider the only other possible explanation: these red gloves were independent agents, beholden to no one, freelance mittens, as it were.

Sauntering along the bitterly cold streets of Marshall,

Saskatchewan, on their way to attend a morning coffee date with friends, these fuzzy hand warmers must have found themselves a mite chilled and chose to pry open the heavy double doors of a random, frigid school bus, clamber inside, and sprawl themselves three rows back, on a glacial vinyl seat.

Yeah, that's it.

One further example of this behavior happened several weeks ago, as a small boy named Randon lifted his arm above the school bus seat to reveal a fat, black, *uncapped* Sharpie, clutched in his paw.

Typically, his response to my loud, immediate query was, "What Sharpie?" But as his seatmate popped into view sporting a thick, misshapen handlebar mustache; heavy, somewhat pointy eyebrows; and two round black circles high on his cheeks, I knew.

We can deny responsibility all we want, but the truth will set us free.

Care to Dance

With school starting soon, I've been thinking about one of the usual curriculum requirements for kids that likely won't be happening this year, owing to the COVID-19 pandemic, namely, the component of dance. Part of the goal in this module is to help kids see the benefit of other forms of fitness, teach them rhythm, encourage them to think creatively, and inspire them to co-ordinate movement with music. Often, depending on the age group participating, dance classes are met with varying degrees of emotion: blissful anticipation, hand-clapping joy, excitement, loathing, dread, or fear.

When I was faced with this grim prospect in the tenth grade, I fell solidly into the last three categories.

I knew only four people in the whole school of at least 600 students, and not one of them was in the gym that morning. However, we were told we had until the next day to pick a partner and choose a song. Then, we were to choreograph some *cool* dance steps for the duration of this tune and perform it for the whole group.

Horrors!

I rode home on the school bus that afternoon thinking desperately of an escape.

Perhaps I could cite some newly found and highly

significant religious convictions prohibiting the frivolous playing of long-play records or repetitive movement?

Maybe I could claim the sudden overnight onset of club foot, or state that irreparable damage had been done to an Achilles tendon after recently having saved an old lady from being hit by a runaway train?

Or what if I blacked out one side of my glasses with a marker and told the teacher that I'd lost an eye after being gored by a bull, as I saved my sibling from certain death?
A girl couldn't be expected to dance if her religious convictions disallowed it, right? Or if she had a disfiguring foot impairment brought on by sacrificial acts of kindness? Or, for sure, if she'd temporarily lost the vision in one eye after saving her little brother, yes?

Apparently not.

With some irritation on the part of our teacher, Irene K. was chosen as my dance partner, and we were sent to a far corner of the stage to think. While Irene was a lovely girl, she didn't know what the heck to do, either, nor were we up-to-date on popular songs.

This was a problem.

The fateful day arrived, and all the other giggling girls performed intricate, coordinated, and ultra-cool moves to their "rockin' tunes." The latest hits reverberated about the room, and everyone swayed along, a blissful smile on each face.

The teacher was pleased, the other students were pleased, heck, even the janitor, peering at us as she swept a nearby floor, was pleased with these girls. And then it was our turn.

Irene strode forward confidently and handed the teacher an album she'd brought from home. I didn't even know what music she'd chosen—let alone consider what dance we'd perform to it—but thought I'd caught sight of several men on the cover wearing heavily embroidered shirts and holding accordions.

Nah, that had to be wrong.

As the record player clicked into position, and the music began to play, Irene grabbed me firmly about the waist, and we clasped clammy hands together, as she hissed, "I'll lead."

And we were off.

The music blared, as the Avsenik Brothers Ensemble launched into one of their better-known polka numbers, and we began a complicated series of maneuvers, made up on the spur of the moment.

Red-faced, we marched clumsily about the room with knees banging together, elbows askew, and muffled apologies murmured, until the last few miserable notes were released from the ivory keys of the lead accordionist—and it was finished.

To say that there was a stunned silence at the conclusion of this event is understating things by quite a bit. Nonetheless, thanks to Irene, Slavko Avsenik, and his band of charismatic brothers, it was done and over—and we breathed a sigh of relief, as we, and the mighty men in embroidered shirts, took our leave.

And so, in answer to the title of this piece: I think I'll sit this one out, thanks.

Two Simple Truths

It was mere hours before my newspaper deadline that I knew what to write in this week's column. Sometimes inspiration is a little hard to come by. However, as I chanced to hear a few momentous words spoken behind me on the school bus, on went the proverbial light.

We'd been rumbling along a dusty grid road after school. A small girl of the world (having newly ascended to the shining pinnacle of the third grade) slumped in her seat, forced to listen to the infinite instructions of an older brother.

He droned on and on, warning her to do her homework, feed the cat, put her lunch box on the counter, blah, blah, blah. Lower and lower she sank in her seat, beaten down by these inexhaustible directions, until suddenly she whirled upon his startled face.

"You're forgetting something," she hissed. "I'm almost done with being seven." She paused to let this weighty statement sink in. "And, I'm the tallest one in my class, so I don't have to listen to your advice anymore."

Properly abashed, her brother fell silent, and she turned dismissively away, wearing a sister's smug smile of victory.

One: Once you reach a certain age (eight years) or height (approximately 3'2"), you may make your own rules in life. Few of us recognize this little-known and mysterious fact. Consider yourself enlightened.

In the first grade class this past week I sat, crisscross-applesauce, with rambunctious students as they listened to the cautionary tale of a young man who made a series of bad choices.

No, he wasn't embezzling funds from a non-profit organization in his poverty-stricken community, or losing his family's farm at the blackjack table—it wasn't that sort of story. This was a lad of six who lived a life of pure, unadulterated impulse.

One little fellow, we'll call him "Johnny," was singularly disinterested in learning the intended lesson.

He wormed his body this way and that, each maneuver calculated to attract maximum attention from his mates.

He slowly stretched each leg perpendicular to the floor. He raised his little arms over his head and waggled fingers, stained with purple marker from coloring the picture of a cat. (Don't ask.)

He lifted himself off the carpet and dropped back into place with a small huffing sound.

Unfortunately, these moves didn't illicit much notice, so he began to speak loudly of video games in an effort to seize control of the class.

"*Shhh*," I remonstrated quietly. With a frown he

subsided, only to broach the fresh topic of recess plans seconds later.

"*Shhh,*" I said a bit louder. He looked away and was silent—for a moment.

Slowly, almost menacingly, he turned to face me, and lifted a pudgy finger to point at lips, still sticky from his recent enjoyment of a pear.

"This is *my* mouth," he ground out from between clenched teeth, "and you can't tell me what to say with it."

Two: Freedom of expression, as outlined in Section Two of the *Canadian Charter of Rights and Freedoms*, is protected, but as was explained to little Johnny in the hallway shortly thereafter, the charter also allows "reasonable" limits to be enforced.

And there you have it: two simple truths laid out for your consideration. Do with them as you see fit.

You're welcome.

Exercise Has Come a Long Way, Baby

It was as I rounded a corner at work that I noticed a teacher hunched furtively outside her classroom door, sternly addressing her upraised arm. She stood alone and held no phone, yet, for some reason, spoke earnestly to a thick black band strapped to her wrist. How peculiar.

Had this woman taken leave of her senses? Gone around the proverbial bend? Felt compelled to re-enact an episode from the 1960s secret agent television parody *Get Smart*? Without the cone of silence and a good dose of truth serum, there was no way to know.

Until I asked her. Turns out, my friend Gwen was dictating text to a device that not only tracks her physical activity and monitors her sleep quality and heart rate, but also links to her cell phone, so she can send and receive messages. *Sheesh*.

With all the recent hoopla over measuring fitness, I, too felt that I should get with the program and downloaded a fitness app to my cell phone. First day of use, I lay groggily in bed, the covers tucked under my chin while I consulted the time and checked for texts.

What the heck? I'd just received a congratulatory message for taking 180 steps prior to 6:00 a.m. But I hadn't even crawled out of bed!

Then later, as I pulled my bus up to the school, I received another admiring notice, praising my continued efforts in taking *six thousand steps* before breakfast! How unreliable was that? It had counted every blessed bump on the road.

Back in the day, I would fling myself around the living room with Jane Fonda and her bevy of cheerful companions to get a workout. No one counted steps then, as I staggered heavily across the shag carpeting. It was all I could do to slog along to the end of the video without collapsing, let alone track how far I went, or how many calories were burned.

Mostly, I tried to exercise in private, though, as my father, who had farmed all of his life, was quite cynical over the relationship Jane and I had. He didn't have much use for such a "foolish waste of energy." To him, only an absolute nut would peddle a bike suspended in midair, or walk endlessly on a treadmill going nowhere fast.

"Get outside and really accomplish something!" he'd shout, as he left for a hard day of work in the fields.

He had strong opinions on weight lifting, too.

"You wanna build your muscles?" he'd bark irritably. "I'll give you weights to lift, by golly! Go spend your day pickin' rocks or haulin' bales. That'll give you a confounded workout."

He'd wave a dismissive hand toward Jane, who leaped spritely about on the nearby TV screen in designer tights and top-quality fitness shoes.

"*Bah!* She wouldn't last five minutes with me," he'd say.

Of course, not every farmer thinks likes him. I knew a man in Manitoba who farmed several thousand acres. Without fail, he'd wake up bright and early every morning and drive to town before sunrise in order to work out at a local gym. He was dedicated. One day, his wife complained to me about it over coffee.

"Sure, it's great that he goes every day," she stated flatly, "but I tell you, he won't even walk twenty steps to the tractor shed. Has to ride the damn quad [bike]. Does that make sense to you?"

It's true that the world has changed—and not just with exercising. Have we come a long way?

You tell me.

Good Taste?

When the news reports are filled with alarming updates and depressing bulletins, I think it's more important than ever to take a moment to relax and breathe. I write this tale in hopes of bringing you that moment.

Recently, I read of a burglar who hunkered down for more than six weeks in the rafters of a Washington state grocery store.

Apparently, the man was discovered when employees of the market complained the legs of an unidentified man had been seen dangling from the ceiling. I can understand that. If I spotted the legs of an unidentified man dangling from the ceiling at my workplace, I'd voice a few complaints, too.

Surveillance video later showed the man skulking through the aisles late at night, dressed in black and filling a large duffel bag with stolen goods from the store, before crawling back into the loft through a vent.

After fours hour of searching the air-circulation system, authorities found the man lurking in a far corner of the ceiling with his latest spoils: twenty-eight cartons of cigarettes and a wheel of artisanal cheese worth $394.97. (Perfect example of fact being stranger than fiction.)

While doubtless a thief and most certainly a trespasser, you have to admit this guy had good taste. Clearly, he didn't choose cheddar, make off with mozzarella, or vamoose with Velveeta. Nope, he crept into the artisanal section of the market and rolled a nearly $400 wheel of Beecher's Handmade Cheese into his sack.

I have to wonder how he'd eventually sell it for profit. Do people buy cheese on the black market?

"*Psst*! Hey, bud," our robber might hiss from a darkened alley, flipping back the front panels of his long black trench coat to reveal several crumbling wedges of Monterey Jack tucked into the inside pockets.

"You wanna buy some cheese?" Then, after a furtive scan of the area for coppers, he'd whisper dramatically, "It's artisanal."

This rather bizarre tale leads me to mention another taste peculiarity I've taken note of within my own family. While I classify it as a peculiarity, my Uncle Dick believes he is, and I quote, "a discerning connoisseur." However, this man, who unashamedly enjoys the occasional peanut butter and onion sandwich *(vile)*, has also acquired a great fondness for the very same snack, but prepared with bologna and raspberry jam.

Although Elvis Presley, too, enjoyed outlandish food combinations such as bacon, peanut butter, and grape jelly sandwiches, I still think it's revolting. Nonetheless, my uncle was quick to defend himself.

"People eat turkey with cranberry sauce all the time, and no one thinks they're crazy," he protested, tearing off another hunk of his preferred snack. "No one gives them a hard time."

To punctuate his remarks, he reached for a bag of Saltine crackers perched beside him at the dinner table, buttered one lavishly, and stuck a single morsel of dog food on top.

"There's not a particle of difference between the two," he finished, deftly tossing the wafer into the drooling mouth of a hound waiting patiently at his feet.

Great. Not only has the man damaged his own taste buds, he's also corrupted the dog's!

Good taste? I think not.

Where the Wild Things Go

As people around the world stay indoors during the 2020 pandemic, wild animals have taken advantage of the peace and quiet. From gangs of turkeys roaming the empty streets of Baton Rouge, Louisiana, to feral Kashmiri mountain goats making their way through the Welsh town of Llandudno, there have been some unusual sightings of late.

Here on the farm, we haven't noticed any difference, which isn't really surprising, particularly considering what I'm about to tell you. As of last fall, when I visited my friend Cyndi in Alberta's capital city of Edmonton, I noticed an interesting fact: there was more wildlife to be seen on the streets of this thriving metropolis than on the lonesome prairie near my home.

Sighting coyotes isn't unusual where I live, but to view them trotting unconcernedly down a city sidewalk in search of one of the juicy jackrabbits that are also prolific in my friend's active neighborhood—well, that's weird. And I haven't seen a jackrabbit in years.

How about this? I like birds, and I walk for miles each spring searching for nests. I slop around sloughs, march in mud, and thrust through thickets in my quest to locate even one lousy duck nest. That shouldn't be too much to ask for, right? But, usually I see nothing, returning home bedraggled and sad.

Now here's the kicker: a mallard duck nested on Cyndi's front lawn, in plain sight, under a cedar—in the middle of flipping Edmonton! There wasn't even any water nearby. When the chicks hatched, they had to cross a busy intersection, tramp past a shopping plaza, waddle behind a Chinese restaurant, and scuttle through a schoolyard to get to a human-made pond in the center of a park. Does this make sense to you?

My friend even has squirrels frolicking in the three trees and six shrubs that have been mandated as backyard landscaping requirements in her area, and their squirrely antics entertain each day. I have great groves of trees everywhere you look on my property, with nary a squirrel to be seen. Or any living creature at all, for that matter, apart from magpies, which I could do well without.

Nonetheless, the *pièce de résistance* happened as I sat at their dinner table and gazed outside at the shredded corner of a sturdy sundeck Cyndi's husband, Darrell, had built. Splinters of wood lay everywhere, covering decorative chairs and a nearby barbecue. Further shards of timber coated the ground below and festooned a flourishing perennial border.

As I turned to ask what had happened, an enormous bird lit on one particularly mangled chunk.

Wow—I was entranced.

I'd only seen such fine fowl in glossy magazines featuring seldom-seen birds, or comprehensive books devoted to the study of our feathered friends.

Then, with a flick of his tail, he gave the remaining wood careful consideration before commencing to hammer upon the battered remains of what had been a lovely ornamental railing.

Woodchips flew.

"Damn bird!" Cyndi yelled, vigorously rapping on the window to shoo him away. "He's been here every day for the past month."

Every day?

I mean, yeah, I guess he did systematically destroy an important component of their home. But, I've never laid eyes on a pileated woodpecker in my whole life. And yet, one flies into the middle of a city, with a population of nearly one million, to brutalize an innocent veranda—every day.

So, the takeaway on this whole situation, as far as I can see, is this: if you want to see wildlife, forget about the countryside—you gotta go to town.

The Family That Slays Together, Stays Together

Due to suspended or slowed production at meat processing plants due to COVID-19 lately, some people have resorted to butchering their own pork and beef. Such a task has been nothing new for country folks throughout history, who did what needed to be done in order to provide for their families, despite the grisly nature of it all.

I saw pictures of such an event on Facebook recently. These people had turned an unpleasant job into a family affair, spending a productive day together as they cut and wrapped the meat and filed it away in freezers.

Perhaps the family that *slays* together, *stays* together? That's a questionable variation on the other well-known phrase, but there may be a grain of truth in it. Who can say?

My husband, Tom, holds fond memories of times he and his mother slaughtered chickens.

"Okay, Helen," he protested, seeing I copied down his precise words for posterity. "Killing chickens didn't exactly create *fond* memories."

He went on to explain that, as a ten-year-old boy, he remembers his mother needing help with the miserable work, and he'd felt proud to be chosen. Even as a child, he understood it was a disagreeable business, but a necessity in order for his family to eat during the winter.

As is often the case with me, I, too, have a memory to share along this unusual theme.

It was 1982. My pretty, young friend Deborah was close to being named Lloydminster Exhibition Queen. It was a prestigious title, as you can well imagine, and highly sought-after. The winner was chosen solely on the number of tickets each girl sold for a car raffle.

Deborah was always far more adventurous and outgoing than I was, and sales were brisk. However, it was a lonely endeavor, and when she asked me to join her one day, I quickly agreed.

Soon, we were traipsing along the streets of a nearby village, stopping at each door with a bright smile and a ticket book bulging with names.

After several long hours, though, we began dragging our feet a little, and when a kindly old lady threw wide her door and beckoned us inside to wait while she gathered her purse, we slid gratefully within.

It was as our eyes adjusted to the dim light that we saw them. A family of perhaps seven adults who turned as of one accord to stare unblinkingly at the two of us, hovering on a mat near the door. Then, without comment nor greeting, they turned their attention back to the matter at hand.

An imposing man, clearly the patriarch, rose slightly

from his seat, and a sharp intake of breath could be heard from the assembled crowd as he raised a long, gleaming blade in the air, paused for a moment of contemplation, then brought it down with force upon the snout of a dead hog that was lying—stiff and unyielding—upon their mahogany coffee table.

Wow!

"Are you girls okay?" the little old lady inquired worriedly. She had returned with the money, but was having trouble pressing it into our frozen hands, or in getting any response from us at all.

"No, we're fine," my friend finally whispered, her gaze riveted on the swinish scene before us. "Thankyouandgoodbye."

She ran the last few words together in an effort to leave hastily but politely. We turned like automatons, our eyes glazed and protuberant, trying *not* to see the bloodthirsty group lean forward to better their view, as the man began sawing energetically at the carcass, slicing down through the jowls with a horrid crunch.

"Did that really happen?" Deborah muttered, once we'd climbed back into her car to recover.

But it had.

See, what did I tell you?

The family that *slays* together, *stays* together

A Burning Desire

Why are human beings so captivated by fire?

Specifically, men—of course. Whether it be a campfire in the wilderness, tending to a barbecue in the backyard, or nursing the perfect blaze within a wood-burning stove, fire tends to fascinate them.

Is it the thrill of creation? An ability to control one of the five elements of nature? Or is it the daredevil aspect of it—dancing with danger, as it were? Let's look at two examples of such behavior and then draw our own conclusions.

The first tale is of a fellow I once knew, who liked—nay, loved—building campfires. A man for whom it had become an art form. Dry leaves were placed at the base, twigs arranged in tepee formation over top, sturdier branches over these, and larger logs placed on the outside.

Then, with a gleam in his eye and a match in his hand, he would urge it into a roaring conflagration before poking it eagerly with more sticks to encourage it higher, and higher, and yet higher, till the leaping flames of this raging inferno were licking the air twenty feet above us. (Slight exaggeration, for effect).

One day, I visited this same man in his home. I recall sniffing the air as I waited on the threshold. Was that a trace of wood smoke I detected on the breeze? I pushed the thought aside as I heard him loudly call from within, "Come on through. I'm a bit tied up at the moment."

Strangely, the smell of smoke became stronger as I opened the door and proceeded down the hallway. My steps quickened. Had a pan of grease gotten the better of him? Did a chicken pie set fire in the oven? Had his fish cakes flambéed?

The poor fellow! I imagined him sturdily standing alone against a rampant fire, struggling to put it out with two damp tea towels and a saucepan of mushroom soup. (It could happen). Good grief! I galloped round the corner in fear for his life, then skidded to a halt.

There he stood, fanning the flames of a mini-campfire built from a bristling bunch of toothpicks on the burner of his stove. A thin line of smoke rose into the air, and through it he smiled sheepishly at me as he toasted an all-beef wiener over the hottest bit.

"Want one?" he asked.

My next illustration is far more recent, but no less outlandish. It involves my husband, Tom, our woodstove (a blameless participant in this story), and an article of men's clothing. On this bitterly cold night, I read while reclining on the sofa.

Suddenly a nasty, acrid smoke assailed my nostrils. It quickly grew worse, forcing me to abandon my cozy spot and seek the clean air of my bedroom. But not before questioning Tom, who had been fiddling with the fire.

"Oh, that?" he said unperturbed, kneeling in the ashes on our hearth. "It's my socks."

"Your *what*?" I asked incredulously. "You burned your socks? On purpose?"

"Yeah. They're brand new, but got holes the first wear, so I thought I'd get a little warmth from 'em, one way or the other."

I glanced beyond him, to where a sizzling heap of polyester burned brightly in the flames.

You be the judge.

Budget Travel 101

The ability to jet across the world on a whim is something we take for granted these days. However, while travel itself has been made easy, the cost often remains high. Of course, there are books teaching us how to see the world on a shoestring, but it doesn't always pay off in the end, or work out quite as easily as we think.

I've done a little of it, experiencing a few of the thrilling highs and crashing lows to be found in budget travel. And, once again, I shall take you along for a glimpse into my European adventures.

Feel free to take notes.

I think a fine place to start would be on the flight. If you've heard that the purchase of noise-canceling headphones is money well spent, I'm here to tell you that it's true. I've listened (against my will) to a married couple argue hotly from Calgary, Alberta, to Glasgow, Scotland, over who ate the last Pop-Tart; heard men sing rollicking Russian tunes across the length and breadth of the Atlantic Ocean; and cringed as children ask loud, embarrassing questions, such as, "Daddy, why does the man beside me smell so bad?"

My advice: get the headphones, or, at the very least, some heavy-duty earplugs.

How about a comfortable, yet cost-effective, hotel for the weary traveler? Wait! Do your research. Our first hotel in Paris looked lovely in the pictures.

Minimalistic? Perhaps.

Austere? Probably.

Yet, though it was clean and the staff friendly, we were warned in halting English not to tarry outside the establishment after dark.

My husband, Tom, was propositioned three times before we figured out why. Yes, I had chosen to take my eight-year-old daughter and indignant husband into an area frequented almost exclusively by "women of the evening."

Another budget hotel had good reviews, but only one person at a time could fit in the tiny, shivering elevator, while the others had to slog up six flights on a staircase so narrow you had to leap onto the handrails to let someone pass.

An economy hotel in Switzerland offered free transit passes, thereby luring me in, but its rooms were more like prison cells than anything. Pale, mint-colored walls led to thin, hard mats arranged in bunk-bed fashion—next to a restroom with a swinging glass door.

Did you catch that last bit?

The adjectives "swinging" and "glass" should *never* describe a bathroom door— anywhere! I'm all for close family relationships, but that crossed the line.

In actual fact, several pages alone could be penned on the subject of restrooms. There was the one in London, where you had to open the door to bend over the sink, and another in Austria, where it was necessary to rise from the potty and stride twelve paces across the room to reach the toilet paper. Still one more in Switzerland was nothing more than a porcelain throne stuck in a broom closet. There wasn't room enough to breathe deeply, let alone drop your drawers. You had to back in from the foyer, trousers round your ankles, butt extended.

"Ah, but was the discomfort worth it," you ask? A thousand times, "Yes!" Where would the adventure have been if everything had gone smoothly?

What funny stories could we tell if there weren't a hitch? Memories are often forged when stuff goes wrong, and we can laugh together later.

And memories are what holidays are all about.

Kind Words

Last week, I felt fortunate to receive a little positive feedback on my stories. It was greatly appreciated. I guess we all wonder, at some point in our lives, what people say about us when we aren't around. Sometimes, it isn't wise to find out, and other times—it can be great.

For me, a perfect instance of this can be traced back to my days driving for Bulldog Corral Cleaning. (Actually, many life lessons can be learned at the base of a manure pile, or at the very least, they can be described by it.)

Yes, it's true: I possess a Class 1 license, allowing me to drive semis, tractor-trailer units, and more. And, there was a time in my life when I used that license to drive a tandem-axle truck, hauling endless loads of manure out of corrals that had housed cattle over our long Canadian winters.

Autumn was always my favorite time at this job. Days were filled with the beauty of the Prairies: crisp morning air; a patchwork quilt of golden leaves against the river hills; silver ribbons of geese winging across a dark, menacing sky; and, of course, a truck filled with steaming mounds of crap.

It seemed there was often a new driver back then, and this day was no exception. An older man had joined our crew that morning, bringing his glowing recommendations along with him. Like most of the fellows who passed through our ranks, his brows raised when he saw me, a woman, then furrowed over his eyes when he was told by Dave W, the boss and owner of the company, that I would be watching him and handing out pointers to the newcomer, if needed. This usually went over like a lead balloon (as my mother used to say), but Dave liked things done a certain way, and he knew I would ensure it was so.

It had gone well enough. We'd worked hard under a blazing sun, and later that evening, everyone was beat as we cleaned our equipment and got ready to load the CAT (a Caterpillar tractor that runs on continuous tracks, rather than on wheels) onto the long trailer.

The new driver was going to pull this trailer with the large and expensive tractor mounted on the back, so he and Dave hurried off to hook up the trailer. It was then that the trouble started.

Since I'd been the last one out to the field with a load, I was the last one back to the yard. As I hopped from my truck and rushed toward the scene, I heard the ominous sound of metal grinding against metal, along with the hoarse hollering of a man exasperated beyond reason.

"Helen could've backed under that hitch with her [*bleepin'*] eyes closed," Dave was shouting. His face red and angry, he gestured vigorously to demonstrate the angle at which the driver should pull forward and try again.

One of the other employees turned to me as I approached and hissed, "The new guy's missed four times. This isn't gonna end well." And it didn't.

Slam!

The truck roared back—almost flattening our boss in the process—and crashed into the trailer, causing it to rock wildly. Dave strode over to the driver's door and ordered the man out.

"Good God! I thought you said you drove trucks all your life?" my boss fumed, leaping behind the wheel to finish the job himself. Then, with one parting shot, he leaned from the window and bellowed, "I'll bet Helen's *backed up* farther than you've driven *forward*!"

Yes, sometimes, if we're very, very lucky, we get to hear good things about ourselves. Even while eavesdropping. Naturally, this didn't endear me to the new driver, and he now hated my slimy guts with an abiding passion, but I was happy.

My boss never gave compliments, so my day had turned out pretty darn fine.

Thanks, Dave.

Gotta Love 'Em

Studies show that the loving relationships people develop with pets can improve their own health, lower stress, and bring joy and pleasure to their lives. Still, there can be an occasional downside.

Take my experiences this week alone. We have three cats (thanks to someone dropping off a pregnant Siamese at our gate) and we love them dearly. However, one of these big, fluffy cats ended up with a bit of a—how do I put this delicately—elimination problem, otherwise known unpleasantly as "fecal matt," in which a lump of excrement becomes enmeshed with the fur on the cat's hind end. Interestingly enough, the Internet holds a plethora of information on this unhappy subject.

While it must be understood that this is no laughing matter, I hooted in disbelief as I read paragraph three, under the heading "Indications of Fecal Matt," which stated that the first clue to its presence might be an unusual odor.

Are you kidding me? I'll say there was an unusual bloody odor!

Paragraph four, with its recommendation to take the cat to a veterinarian and submit your pet to a rigorous physical examination—in order to obtain a definitive diagnosis—was completely unnecessary.

Next: treatment.

Ever tried submerging a cat's butt in a tub of warm water and melting down a crusted lump of poo from his rear end? It ain't no picnic, people. My daughter helped by holding his front parts, complete with gnashing teeth and slashing claws, while I held his lacerating back legs with one hand, and wiped and snipped the offending brown matter away with the other.

I can tell you that the yowling, screeching, and whining that ensued during this miserable task was absolutely *unbelievable* (and the cat put up quite a fuss, too).

The next day, Chili, our dog, appeared at the door with a muzzle full of porcupine quills. *Great.* I managed to hold her long enough to pull out a few, but she fought so hard that I waited for my husband, Tom, to arrive home for the rest.

Groaning with exertion, he wrestled her across the kitchen floor, as she scraped and writhed and struggled in vain to escape us. But, I managed to pull every quill. Even a few that had lodged themselves in her gums—*Ouch*!

Now, if these tales of woe cause you alarm when thinking of owning a cat or a dog yourself, be of good cheer. According to a recent TV news report, there is a somewhat unorthodox alternative available at a Vancouver animal shelter.

You could adopt a rat.

And not just any old gutter rat, scrabbling around in nameless filth. These are "fancy rats." However, keep in mind that not every fool walking through the door is allowed to adopt vermin. Rats have standards. But, if you offer a loving home, pay your five-dollar fee, and have your rodent spayed or neutered, you're in.

The benefits are endless, too, as I read these rodents are friendly, enjoy human, companionship, and make great pets for children. Just ask the roughly fifty million people who died of the bubonic plague. Oh right, you can't—'cause they're *dead*. (Yes, I know they lived in the fourteenth century. That's beside the point.)

Foolishness aside, pets of any shape or size (except snakes) can be beneficial to one's life and one's happiness, and I'm all for it. Just remember to be responsible and be prepared to provide them with health care, nourishment, love, companionship, and a forever home. They will pay you back many, many times over.

(But not snakes.)

Start Your Engines!

And so, with a mighty roar of engines and a fastidious check of lights and equipment, buses spring to life once more and herald the beginning of another school year.

Hooray!

In my mind's eye, I envision bright-eyed, rosy-cheeked children clambering up the steps with a glad cry on their lips and a delighted spring in their steps. This may be a slight exaggeration—okay, a big one—but I think kids are generally happy to return. I know I am. While having no wish to belabor the back-to-school theme, I thought I might share with you an excerpt or two from the time I've spent behind the wheel.

Often, I'm asked if driving the same country roads each day becomes boring or tedious.

In a word, "No."

A variety of sights are sure to be spotted if you "keep your eyes peeled," as my mother used to say.

One morning in particular, the parade of Canadian wildlife that filed past our windows almost seemed like an orchestrated event. It began as several moose trotted peacefully down the road in front of the bus before lightly springing over a fence and vanishing into a bluff. A bald eagle peered at us from his lofty perch in a pine above as we motored past, and two foxes streaked across our path, their coats blazing red in the morning sun.

Then, a skunk, his plume-like tail waving to and fro, disappeared down into the long grass beside us (we gave him a wide berth), and a badger ambled across a summer fallow field and dove into the thick underbrush. However, the showpiece was spotting a small herd of antelope.

The kids and I were on high alert by this time, and I pulled over and stopped, allowing everyone to stand at the windows and gape at them. It was quite an unusual sight for us, and the kids were reluctant to resume their seats and continue on to school after all the excitement of the trip.

One youngster paused beside me as he exited the bus at the school and observed with amazement, "Holy, Mrs. Toews. Riding on your bus is like taking a drive through the zoo!"

Before I became an education assistant at my local school, I was exclusively a bus driver, and it was the sole interaction I had with the kids. I've fielded some humorous questions and heard some funny remarks over the years, as I know all who work with children do.

One such time was toward the end of a school year. A little girl had begun taking the bus each day for her first grade class, and she sat sweetly behind me swinging her legs and making light conversation.

She was the first one on and the last one off, so we spent

a lot of time mulling over critical matters of state, things like what is sand made of, how her new sparkly shoes looked in the sun, why cats throw up—important stuff.

One Saturday, I happened to meet this family in the local shopping mall. The little girl scurried around behind her mother as we spoke and peeked out from behind mom's legs. She hadn't seen me outside the confines of a bus, and I supposed it was a bit overwhelming for her.

Her eyes widened with apprehension, and she refused to speak when I referred to our last conversation concerning the bowl habits of their new puppy.

After passing a few polite pleasantries with her parents, we parted, and I laughed all the way to my car when I heard her whine loudly to her folks, "But, Mom, I was scared. I didn't know she could *walk*!"

Yes, I anticipate a great year ahead filled with learning and adventure. Driving kids to and from school is an important job, and we bus drivers take it very seriously. Each one of the kids becomes an important part of our day, and I miss them a lot when they grow up and move on.

Here's to education!

Learning From Our Mistakes?

The season for holidaying in countries that have temperate climates is now winding down. Kids are back in school, harvest has begun in earnest, and we must gear up to handle another frigid six months of winter.

Some lucky folks already have plans for an escape to warmer temperatures, but I only have those extra pounds I gained in Paris this spring to keep me warm. Of course, I have memories to content myself with—bringing me to the purpose of this story today.

One can't help but learn valuable information each time they travel, and while mine may never rival those of author Rick Steves (personal hero), I have a couple of points to share, which may prove enlightening.

When in Rome with family last year, we were directed to a restaurant by an enthusiastic local. It was so authentically Italian that no one there could speak a word of English. Around 8:00 p.m., people stared to pour through the door in a boisterous stream, lively discussions with plenty of arm-waving ensued, and tables of happy Italians spilled out onto the street.

Orange flames leaped from a wood-fired oven in the corner, and bright checked tablecloths welcomed guests who were eager to eat.

We were ushered to a spot in the center of the room, where clearly we were an oddity. Interested stares followed our conversation and our halted attempts to order from the menu. When my turn arrived, I looked nervously into the uncomprehending face of the waitress. Jabbing a finger at the only word I understood—"mozzarella"—I nodded encouragingly.

How wrong could I go choosing an item featuring cheese? She raised an inquiring eyebrow, but quickly schooled her features as she moved along.

Melanie, my daughter-in-law, was thirsty. "I'll have a tall glass of lemonade," she said brightly, pointing to another item on the list, *limoncello*. How was she to know it wasn't lemonade at all, but an after-dinner digestive averaging twenty-six percent alcohol?

Entirely unprepared, she took a deep swig from the pretty chilled glass and recoiled backward onto her chair, choking and spluttering.

More odd looks.

Finally, our food arrived, and mine was plunked before me. Nestling wetly in a bed of pale, shaved lettuce was a glistening ball of cheese.

That's it—nothing else. Just a glob of cheese. In disbelief, I studied the gelatinous orb for a moment before picking up a fork and poking it suspiciously.

This was supper? Fabulous.

Poising my utensils over its shining flesh, I sliced. It squished audibly like a sponge wrung out in the bath. Streams of liquid spurted unpleasantly from its sides, and soon the greens floated in a vast pool of opaque white fluid. I may have been raised on fresh cow's milk, but this was ridiculous.

My family hooted at me in laughter, their mouths filled with delicious pizza.

Buon appetito, Helen, you nut!

Tip Number One: Consult a pocket translator before ordering; next time it could be *cervelli fritti* (calf brains).

In France this past April, my friend Susan and I toured the fabulous Palace of Versailles, home of King Louis XIV. It's popular to visit at any time of year, so we rose early, rushed out of our apartment without a bite to eat, and boarded a train, hoping to beat the rush.

It was not to be. We arrived at the gates to find several hundred people ahead of us.

Crestfallen, we stood on the cobblestones until I remembered that taking a private tour of the king's apartments would avoid the queue! Minutes later we began the visit, but the morning had taken its toll on my pal.

Susan felt faint.

The air was heavy and oppressive as we trudged through each opulent room. We saw the library, Louis's personal dining area, and a large space dedicated to his clothes. (My friend was fading, but unwilling to quit.)

We traversed the games room, the clock room, and made it through an apartment set aside for the king's hounds, but it was as we entered his lavish sleeping quarters my comrade walked unsteadily to an open window and clutched at the sill in an effort to find fresh air.

Immediately, an attractive guard was at her side with a chair, inquiring in broken English if he could be of assistance. Additional emergency personnel (all male) were radioed and attended her closely—each one ruggedly good-looking.

They clustered about her with concern.

Despite Susan's protests, they helped my chum to stand, and flanking her closely on either side, led her from the room, where her hand was held consolingly and she was plied with fruit and chocolate to revive her failing strength.

Ultimately, my friend was fine, apart from low blood sugar, but her timing was perfection itself.

Tip Number Two: Feeling faint? Swooning in the king's bedchamber, surrounded by dashing young male security guards, is the only way to go.

When we're open to advice, it's possible to learn from the mistakes other travelers have made. There's plenty of information in travel books, on the Internet, and from folks who've been there personally to help us avoid such incidents and make the most of our time.

However, if everything always went perfectly, there wouldn't be a memorable story to recall, and sometimes lessons can't be taught by example.

Sometimes, such as in this last example, they're only acquired by trial and error, making the same blunder several times, over and over—repeatedly — if you catch my drift?

You with me, Sue?

What a Game!

Autumn signals the beginning of school sports, and of them, volleyball remains my favorite. I always enjoyed playing and, oddly enough, was voted team captain in the ninth grade. I say oddly, because I wasn't a great player, nor did I possess strong leadership qualities. To be honest, I barely understood the rules. No, as I was informed later, it was because I was considered "nice." Don't get me wrong, that's fine and all, but it's hardly the basis on which to build a winning team.

The first match we ever played was in the nearby hamlet of Hillmond, Saskatchewan. Their school had a real gym. For a group of girls who learned to play in a clay pit, dug from the side of a hill behind the school, this space was pretty elaborate. There were even bleachers—and spectators.

Yikes.

Looking awed, our team trailed in wearing the usual blue jeans and sneakers, while the other team sprinted on to the court in matching uniforms.

I don't remember who won, although I could hazard a guess. Nope, what stands out in my memory was the fact that I played the first two sets with a serious wardrobe malfunction. My face burned with shame when a concerned mother finally told me. There I'd been, leaping, serving, spiking, and volleying—all with the fly of my pants down.

Of course, soccer's a great sport, too. While recently watching kids aged six to eight who were struggling to learn the rudiments of this game, I thought how lucky I was to be witness to such an event. It convinced me to try my hand at sports commentating, in order to share a few glorious moments with you.

Listen up.

Surrounding the teacher in the gym that day, thirteen eager faces watched with rapt attention as he explained the rules, while a further nine weren't the slightest bit interested: one twiddled his hair; three whispered in a huddled group; another pulled threads from his shirt; and still more lay on the floor, staring sightlessly into the rafters.

Rules are for chumps. You don't need rules when, regardless of the game being played, you run around in circles, screaming like banshees.

The game begins: Johnny is in goal for team Yellow, straining to see who has the ball. An angry mob fights for it mere inches away.

Wait!

That angry mob are all members of the same team—his! What's going on?

They scrap over the ball amid shouts of, "Give it here" and "I had it first!"

Hang on—team Yellow has a breakaway. The player

runs, he feigns, he dodges, he draws back, and boots the ball as hard as he can.

He scores!

Red-faced, Johnny shouts at him, "WHADYA THINK YOU'RE DOIN'?" but his teammate turns with a shrug. Who cares if he scored on his own team—he got a *goal*.

Play continues: Johnny scans the area for a teammate *other* than the kid who just scored and passes the ball so hard he falls over backward.

Correction, that wasn't a pass: he tripped on someone's toy car. How did that get here, for heaven's sake?

Meanwhile, the ball slams into the ankle of a Red team player as she shows friends how to perform a new dance move at center field. Irritably, she kicks it away.

"Leave me alone," she yells, before turning back to her friends who, in her absence, have been practicing their twirls, just like she showed them.

Back to the action: Yellow swarms the ball again. Oh no—several of the players have fallen over someone who appears to have lain down on the playing field to rest. What the heck? The ball rolls away.

"Stand up and play the game!" the teacher roars from the sidelines.

The ball is in play again. Hang on, folks. An argument

has broken out near the Red team's goal.

"It's my turn to have it!" Sammy, on team Red cries, snatching the ball to his chest.

A crowd quickly gathers to determine if it really is Sammy's turn, when, from nowhere in particular, a Yellow player slams into Sammy for a steal (Or was she just shoved by someone running hurriedly to the potty?,) the ball tumbles from the boy's grasp, then meanders past the goalposts. It's another goal!

(Yellow team cheers uproariously.)

In truth, it would have been an easy save for Red, if the goalie had been watching any of the action. Unfortunately, he'd been standing with his back to the game for the past five minutes, arguing with a teammate over who'd eaten the biggest apple at lunch.

No matter. The match has ended in a tie, and everyone races to be first at the water fountain.

What a game!

Things That Go Squeak!

Bar your doors! This is the time of year when assorted vermin, looking for warm winter dwellings, squeeze through little cracks or crannies and enter our country homes. It can pose an unpleasant annoyance or a huge challenge, depending on the varmint.

An invasion of a mouse or two is the most likely. Some folks say to keep a cat, as the mere smell of them will ward off mice.

Not true.

While keeping a cat is effective in the long run, it's a lengthy, unpleasant process of elimination involving much repartee between both parties, and always ending messily.

Others say placing a bar of highly scented soap near doorways or other entries will keep them at bay.

Also untrue.

I watched with my own two beady little eyes as a mouse scooted in the door, while I struggled to bring in a load of laundry. Knowing I'd placed some soap nearby as a deterrent, I watched with trepidation.

He ran up to the lurid green cleanser—which promises the user thereof a malodorous spring day—mounted its slippery slope, and turned for a wee moment to glance back, his tiny claws gripping the mass with ease and apparent unconcern.

Was he pausing to usher in his pregnant wife and extended family members? Or was he simply signaling, in some mouse brand of communication, "Follow me, men. The coast is clear, and the way is paved with green perfume."

In autumn 2014, the CBC reported on a Regina area home, where more than 300 snakes had been removed.

How horrible!

In my travels around the countryside, it seems to me there are more garter snakes now than ever before, but can you imagine an infestation in your home?

Sorry, I'm not fond of snakes. And I've had a long history of dealings with the slithering reptiles. One such incident involves me, my television, a broom, two snakes, and a lot of bloody- awful hollering. Yes, I know they catch mice and are harmless creatures. I still don't like them.

In the CBC article, it was noted that, of the 300 snakes re-homed, four had "health issues" that required attention. These included an eye infection, broken vertebrae, and unexplained sluggishness. Sluggishness would have been the least of their worries if I'd have found 300 snakes in *my* basement, I can assure you.

(In actual fact, I'd have probably hopped the next bus out of town.)

Late in October of last year, we arrived home from a shopping expedition with our little dog, Trixy, a Jack Russell terrier. My daughter Aliyah carried her sedately in the door, whereupon Trixy sniffed the air and began pedaling wildly in her arms, straining to be free.

Surprised, Aliyah set her down, and she tore off around the corner. Thinking little of this outburst, since our diminutive dog leans toward the hyperactive, I began to put away the groceries. Moments later, I heard her yelp, my husband Tom shout, and complete pandemonium break out.

Sounds of furniture being dragged, rushing footsteps, claws skittering on lino, snapping, yelping, barking, and general chaos ensued. I stood, rooted to the spot, listening as Tom attempted to curb the actions of our small, bloodthirsty pooch.

Dashing from the scene of the action, Aliyah charged toward me with wide- eyed amazement and delivered the fateful words, "It's a weasel!"

"What?" I yelled, hastily clambering onto a chair. My brave daughter hopped on one as well, and we stood, peering toward the trouble from our elevated positions, awaiting the outcome.

It was all over in minutes.

Trixy had the time of her life. The same cannot be said for the weasel. Clearly, he acted on poor instinct indeed when choosing to enter the home of a terrier.

It was unfortunate, as I quite like weasels. How he got there, or why he came, I shall never know, but one thing I can be sure of: this time of year, we country dwellers sometimes have unexpected visitors in our homes.

Be on the alert.

Many Thanks

Although recent weather may leave us struggling to be thankful, I must share two more items for which I am personally grateful during this Thanksgiving time of year.

Kids: This fall, I have a new girl riding on my school bus. With wisdom gleaned from six long years on Earth, Sophie busily informed Carson (my oldest passenger) how to accurately color a star, discussing at length the merits of wax versus pencil and furnishing him with detailed instructions on how best to stay within the lines.

Sophie also took time out of her busy schedule to specify the correct driving technique I should employ when entering her yard and rendered a brief lesson on properly identifying a duck. These are valuable insights, as you can well imagine, but her last pronouncement was the clincher.

On the afternoon in question, with very few children aboard, I had allowed her to sit in the back seat. For those of you who are unaware, the back seat of a school bus is a prestigious place to be, tantamount to being knighted by the queen of England or named the king of Siam for a day.

Sophie's shiny auburn hair danced as she scurried along the aisle with glee and disappeared from view. After a short trip to her house, I applied the brake and turned to watch her skip toward me. Small teeth flashed like a tiny row of pearls across her flushed face as she paused, her blue eyes wide with excitement, and broadly grinned.

Then, drawing a deep breath, she exclaimed with profound emotion, "That was so much fun, I almost puked!"

Thank goodness for little girls.

Fathers: Dad has an ancient root cellar beneath a shed in the yard, where he keeps potatoes throughout the winter. However, the steps leading into this subterranean pit are aged and steep, causing me concern lest he stumble and lie undetected in a crumpled heap at the bottom.

The other day, finding him with a pail on his way to this miserable pit for spuds, I insisted that if anyone was going to lie in a crumpled heap, it should be me.

Reaching for the old iron handle, Dad hauled up the heavy wooden door, which gave a protesting creak. Carefully, I descended into the murky depths, my mind reeling with thoughts of spiders, mice, and the ubiquitous snake. Over the years, we've had a problem with these slithering reptiles. I *hate* them.

Nonetheless, I reached bottom and squinted into the gloom.

"Hey, you need a light," Dad yelled helpfully, voicing the obvious. "Wait here." And dropping the heavy lid into place with a thick shower of dust, he clumped from the shed, slammed the door, and was gone.

"Well, this is a fine bloody thing," I said crossly into the musty black hole. "Of course I have to wait. I'm trapped in the pit of doom!"

Time passed.

Did something just glide across my foot, I thought fearfully?

Do I hear rustling on my right?

I stood, shivering in the dark void, clutching the plastic pail to my chest.

Where was the man? Had he gone for refreshments? Perhaps slipped into the house for a quick rest before commencing the tiresome search for a flashlight? I imagined him, coffee in hand, seated comfortably at the table reading the newspaper.

Suddenly, I remembered my phone. Hurriedly, I flipped it on and beamed it cautiously around the earthy walls. There, stretched up high, not two feet from my boot, was a coiled garter snake, its glittering eyes fixed on my throat (small exaggeration) and its forked tongue flicking the air. Testing the waters, so to speak, before it struck at my defenseless limbs.

Just then, Dad pulled up the lid, and I must say, with all my heart, "Thank goodness for fathers.

There's always something to be grateful for."

Happy Thanksgiving Day!

A Place in the Sun

When gale-force winds wind themselves around the granaries, and temperatures dip below what any sensible person would go out in, more and more people think of escaping to the South. And there are so many possible destinations.

In the past, such a pursuit was something only the prosperous could afford, and these affluent people enjoyed the privilege of being a seasonal resident. Even during the Victorian era, wealthy Europeans and residents of the U.K. would flee the winter cold of the North, as they journeyed toward the Mediterranean, where the climate was milder.

Naturally, owning or renting a home in a warmer climate is only one way to escape frigid temperatures. Almost everyone you talk to these days has been somewhere tropical for a winter holiday. The allure of an all-inclusive vacation, where one can briefly escape the snow and cold, creates a compelling reason to make exit plans forthwith.

Sadly, I've never gone anywhere warm during the winter. Unless making a trip to the sofa with an electric heater and a blanket would count?

No? I didn't think so.

Along this line of thought, I often indulge myself in a

little pipe dream—*fade to black*.

As the curtain rises, I see myself basking in the bright sunshine of a January morning on the French Riviera. At my back is a small rustic dwelling, nothing too ostentatious, you understand. Just a simple six-bedroom home facing the Côte d'Azur. As I gaze over the gently lapping waves of the Mediterranean, a small, almost scornful smile, lights my face and several questions are pondered.

Is there a snowdrift in sight? Frost in the air? Ice underfoot?

"No!" I cry, with a joyous fist pump, accidentally dropping the keys to my red Porsche into the infinity pool.

Usually, at this point, a humble pot of potatoes boils over on the stove, or the cat claws my leg wanting kibble, and I'm jolted back to reality at home in Canada.

Sigh.

In any case, I've taken certain steps to be ready, on the off-chance that this is my true destiny. Spending the last three years learning to speak French, with the help of a couple of online courses, I now feel equipped to handle any situation that may surface while living abroad.

It's hard to envision when I might need to say, "A lion is among the crowd," or "This white hat does not suit my grandmother," but if, while in France, circumstances require me to warn the masses of an impending lion attack, or my grandmother is found alive and poorly dressed in a women's accessory shop, I've got it covered.

With all of this in mind, I congratulate those of you fortunate enough to jet off through the snowstorm and land elsewhere in a greener pasture—far, far away. Enjoy your moments of pleasure under the radiant sun in some exotic land, while the rest of us poor slobs grimly advance into another glacial morning, yanking open the squealing doors of our vehicles to huddle miserably inside.

We'll be fine—enjoy yourselves.

Holiday Rituals

Have you, at any time, wondered where Christmas symbols and customs came from? Ever questioned the wisdom—or sanity—in erecting a six-foot fir tree in the living room? And for what purpose do we garnish said tree in lights and baubles, only to pleasurably watch as it slowly shrivels to a husk?

What strange force compels us to smooch under a sprig of greenery suspended from the ceiling, and why, pray tell, do we hang old socks on the mantle? For the answers to these and other burning inquiries, stay tuned.

This is your lucky day!

The thought process began for me this year as I dragged a pine tree into my house via the front door. The hinges complained bitterly as it squeezed past, and if we could but ask it, I'm sure the tree was none too happy over this bizarre turn of events, either.

So, why do we follow this curious ritual each year? It turns out no one is positive when trees were first used for Christmas celebrations, but estimates put it in Northern Europe about 1510. According to *whychristmas.com*, a group of local unmarried merchants, called the "Brotherhood of Blackheads," placed a tree in the town square, pranced around it in a lively fashion, then set it ablaze. (This information conjures up unpleasant images on several levels.)

Perhaps the first person to actually bring a tree inside a dwelling was Martin Luther in the sixteenth century. Apparently, one December evening, the German preacher was returning home through the forest and noticed how brightly the stars twinkled between the branches. This event inspired him to replicate the effect using candles on the branches of a tree he brought inside his own household.

Nice idea—logistical nightmare.

Later on, Queen Victoria's husband, Prince Albert of Germany, brought the custom of the Christmas tree to England, and it spread from there.

Another tradition, which came from England, was kissing under the mistletoe; although, its roots were in Norse mythology. Likely, due to the fact it could bloom despite the cold temperatures of winter, mistletoe came to be seen as a symbol of vigor and fertility. It represented peace, love, and friendship, and those who kissed beneath it had the hope of good luck and contentment throughout the following year.

The name is derived from two Anglo-Saxon words: *mistel*, which, unfortunately, means "manure," and *tan*, which means "twig" or "branch." I'll let you put that together on your own.

Moving right along we come to stockings "hung by the chimney with care." As is the case with most traditions, there's no real record of when or how this ritual came to be. The version most commonly told is of a widowed father struggling to marry off his three daughters. (No doubt, the expense of keeping them in gowns and girdles was substantial.)

During this time in history, girls required a significant dowry to lure men into the bonds of matrimony; these girls had none. Mercifully, ole St. Nicholas heard of their plight and decided to help. Interestingly enough, there are two conflicting endings to this tale, both of them equally far-fetched, and one of them involving a clear case of break and enter.

The first ending states, for some inexplicable reason, that St. Nicholas handily scaled the family's residence while they slumbered and then dropped in through the chimney.

Heavy, hobnailed boots noiselessly navigating the roof, he must have ascended the peak and soundlessly plummeted two stories into the fire below, and by some stroke of luck, never alerted the family to his presence.

Admirable fellow!

Discovering their stockings hung to dry, he filled them with gold coins. Presumably, he then trod out the front door, or, more in keeping with his stealthy ways, perhaps jimmied the window, seeking exit.

The other conclusion sees him flinging (with remarkable accuracy) three bundles of gold coinage down the chimney, late at night, while galloping past their humble home on his splendid white steed. Naturally, each sack of money was dropped fortuitously into a sock hung on the mantle below.

Use your imagination—it could happen.

When examined closely (and with tongue-in-cheek), some long-held traditions may appear a bit odd, but they are merely the trappings of this glorious time of year.

What is important are the people we hold dear to our hearts and the happiness and love we share with them. Agreed?

A Christmas Carol

If, during time spent with family and friends this holiday season, you find yourself playing a rousing game of Trivial Pursuit, please take heed. It may seem unlikely now, but the following question could well be posed: "How many times can the first two lines of 'Rudolph the Red-Nosed Reindeer' be heard before a perfectly sane individual goes mad?"

I have the answer: exactly eighty-three.

I gained this knowledge from personal experience. Rolling down the road in my school bus, I listened one day as the first twenty-two performances of this tune were warbled aloud. I smiled indulgently into my rearview mirror at the reflection of a sweet little girl, who sang serenely behind me, her soft brown eyes aglow with the love of Christmas.

What a pretty voice she had. Then, as a further twenty-six renditions were sung without pause, my smile became somewhat wooden, and my eyes began to—ever so slightly—bulge.

However, it was that final thirty-five that really tipped me over the edge into a realm of near hysteria. Well—not really—but it was close!

I find kids these days don't know as many Christmas

carols as they once did. Oh sure, they know the aforementioned refrain, immortalizing the plight of an unpopular deer and his fickle companions.

And they're well acquainted with one that follows the antics of a snowman on a harrowing afternoon spent in the company of some rowdy kids, a lot of sunshine, and a traffic cop, but I'm referring to the old carols we used to sing.

During the last two weeks of school before the holiday break, kids at my school are treated to a game called "Name That Tune."

One verse from a Christmas song is played over the intercom each morning, and children are invited to guess what it is. Carefully, they scrawl the most outlandish ideas on to bits of paper and submit them to the office, where the correct ones are entered in the draw for a daily, edible prize.

Naturally, children in the younger grades are at a bit of a disadvantage, so there's always a selection of easy ones played for them. That's when titles like "Lettel Poor Jeesis" and "Yo, Babee of God" are brought confidently forth.

Several years ago, I was standing in the first grade classroom when a few lines of "Away in a Manger" were played. No one knew what it was called. Small bodies shuffled uneasily, and pencils began to scratch out the usual wild guesses. A lot was at stake, since the winner walked off with a delicious chocolate treat. One pint-sized fellow sat at his desk, agonizing over a scrap of paper.

"MAN! What is it?" he fussed, squinting heavenward, as

if seeking divine intervention.

Finally, as time ran out, he hastily scribbled a few words, folded the paper, and sent it off to be judged. He then slumped at his desk, listening for the winner to be announced.

When the bitter blow arrived (in the form of a correct answer, which wasn't his), he flopped backward on his seat dramatically. Deeply aggrieved, he punched a fist into his chubby little hand and shook his head regretfully, "I gotta get out to church more!" he exclaimed with a frown. "I coulda used that chocolate."

As far as the old, time-honored Christmas carols go, we can help keep them alive as individuals and families, should we so choose. I cherish times spent with my loved ones and a guitar, as we gather together to sing on a cold winter's night during the Christmas season.

Just one fervent request for this year, though, please: no tunes about Rudolph, okay?

Oh, Christmas Tree

Today, our school principal shared a humorous memory of Christmas trees gone wrong. Funny how it's always the bad experiences we recall the best. Since it's the time of year for such reminiscence, I thought I'd share one of mine with you.

Snow swirled outside the frosty windowpanes of my childhood home, and dark clouds hung ominously in the sky. It was 1975. A winter storm had raged the night before, but our old cook-stove blazed within, and we were toasty warm as our family met in the kitchen for breakfast. Today, we were to drive into Lloydminster, Saskatchewan, and purchase our holiday tree. Little brother, Bill, and I were excited.

"We aren't going to get a Christmas tree this year," Dad stated, as he stirred honey into his bowl of steaming porridge. Quickly, he held up a hand to silence our protests. "Buying a tree that just gets tossed away is like throwing good money to the wind. I've got a better idea."

With long faces, Bill and I stared at each other. What did he mean no tree? It was unthinkable.

After eating, we watched as Dad pulled on his heavy work clothes and bent to pick up an evil-looking handsaw he'd left beside his boots. Wordlessly, he flung open the door and set off through the deep snow toward a line of firs near the bull's pen.

Presently he reappeared, dragging what looked like a tall tree behind him. Breathlessly, I turned from the doorway to tell Bill.

"That's no tree," he said dryly, clambering onto a chair to look out a window. "It's a fat branch."

And so it was.

Proudly, Dad dragged it into the house and, with no small effort, strapped it to the living-room wall using several yards of binder twine and a box of nails.

How festive.

Later that evening, feeling pleased with himself, Dad proposed a toast.

"Let's celebrate with eggnog," he said, rubbing his hands together with invisible soap. No doubt about it, the man was on a roll. Earlier that day, he'd happily presented Mom with a blender—a pre-Christmas gift.

She'd been absolutely thrilled! What woman wouldn't? (Our family may be frugal, but sarcasm's free.)

Dad tugged the shiny new appliance from its box, fit the glass container into position, and began adding the ingredients he'd found listed in an included recipe. With a flourish, he pressed the *On* button, the machine sprang to life, and the assembled family broke into spontaneous applause. (We're simple folk and easily amused.)

As our eagerly anticipated beverage spun to a halt, Dad handed out glasses, grasped the handle, and hoisted it on high.

Kersplash!

The bottom portion of the jug and its contents gushed forth, spraying the floor, the dog, and our feet with ice-cold eggnog.

Dad hadn't tightened the bottom.

And so, as we gathered round our scrawny Christmas branch that evening and gazed at the brightly wrapped gifts shoved against the wall, we raised celebratory glasses of water to clink together with joy.

After all, it's not about the tree, the gifts, or the food—it's about love.

Christmas on the Ranch

'Twas the night before Christmas, all over the ranch,
Not a creature was stirring—it seemed at first glance.
The children were nestled all snug in their beds,
While visions of taco chips danced in their heads.

The stockings were flung on the back of a chair,
In hopes that ole Santa would notice them there.
And Papa with his soda, and I with my tea,
Had just settled down on the couch, by the tree.

When out on the lawn there arose such a clatter,
I sprang from my seat yelling, "Now what's the matter!"
Away to the window I flew like a flash,
Knocked over Tom's Pepsi and fell with a crash!

Then what to my wondering eyes should appear,
But a miniature sleigh and one Charolais steer.
With a little old driver, so short and so plump,
I knew that he couldn't see over its rump.

More rapid than turtles they plodded along.
Though he whistled and shouted and hollered this song:
"My reindeer are missing, and all I could find
Was this lumbering steer and his massive behind."

To the top of the porch, to the top of the wall,
The cumbersome steer put a hoof through them all.
He soared to the rooftop in one mighty leap,
But then lost his footing! The roof—it's too steep!

In only a twinkling I heard something slip.
As Santa, the sleigh, and the steer lost their grip.
I drew in my head and was turning around,
To see the whole works of them fall to the ground.

He was dressed all in fur, from his head to his toe,
And he yelled, "Damn that beast that I got from Les Row."
He was jolly-well mad—a right angry old elf—
And I shook by the window in spite of myself.

But, a wink of his eye and a nod of his head,
Soon gave me to know I had nothing to dread.
He had a broad face and a round little belly
That shook when he ran, to evade our dog Kelly.

He picked up the toys and turned over the sleigh,
Then growled at the animal, "Stay there, okay!"
A bundle of toys he then tossed on his back,
And he rounded the house, sneaking in through the back.

His eyes, how they twinkled. His dimples, how merry.
He gummed down a cookie and sighed, "That was scary."
A stump of a pipe he held tight in his teeth,
Though the smoke was so putrid it wilted my wreath.

His droll little mouth was drawn up in a bow,
And he tracked in some dirt—'cause we didn't have snow.
He mumbled a bit, but went straight to his work.
And filled all the stockings, then turned with a smirk.

And laying a finger aside of his nose,
He glanced out the window and suddenly froze.
For there in the moonlight he saw that his sleigh
Was rounding a corner and flying away.

He sprang down the steps and ran out of the dwelling.
He woke up the children with all of his yelling.
But I heard him exclaim, ere he puffed out of sight:
"You'll pay for this, Les, if it takes me all night!"

Helen Row Toews is a writer, works in education, and
carries a license to drive anything on wheels
(stilettos and lipstick optional).

Living on the family farm near Marshall, Saskatchewan,
Helen shares her love of the Canadian Prairies, family,
travel and country living—all humorously woven into
the fabric of these memorable tales. Her fondest wish
is to bring a smile to your face.

Another Prairie Wool Book by Helen Row Toews,
Is It Just Me?

Life can get a little crazy when: your job leaves you
with a mouthful of cow manure, you're mistaken
for a hooker in a prestigious clothing store, or your
redneck uncle forces you to sing at the optician's
office for a ten percent discount.

Manufactured by Amazon.ca
Bolton, ON